SARAH CAIN MUSIC BOOK

THE FRANCES YOUNG TANG TEACHING MUSEUM AND ART GALLERY
SKIDMORE COLLEGE

X ARTISTS' BOOKS

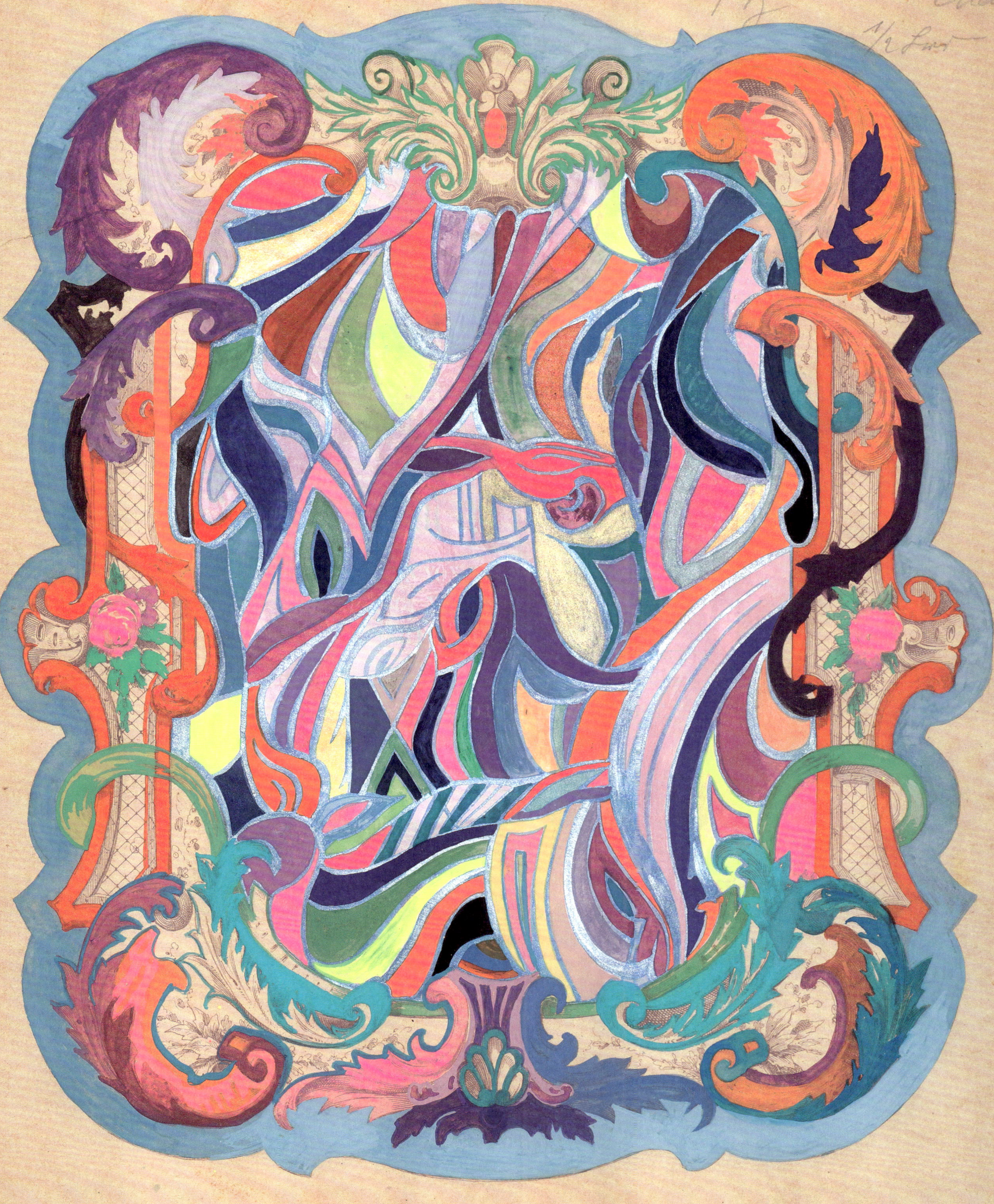

Georg-Marsch.

Einleitung.

Aug. Herzog.

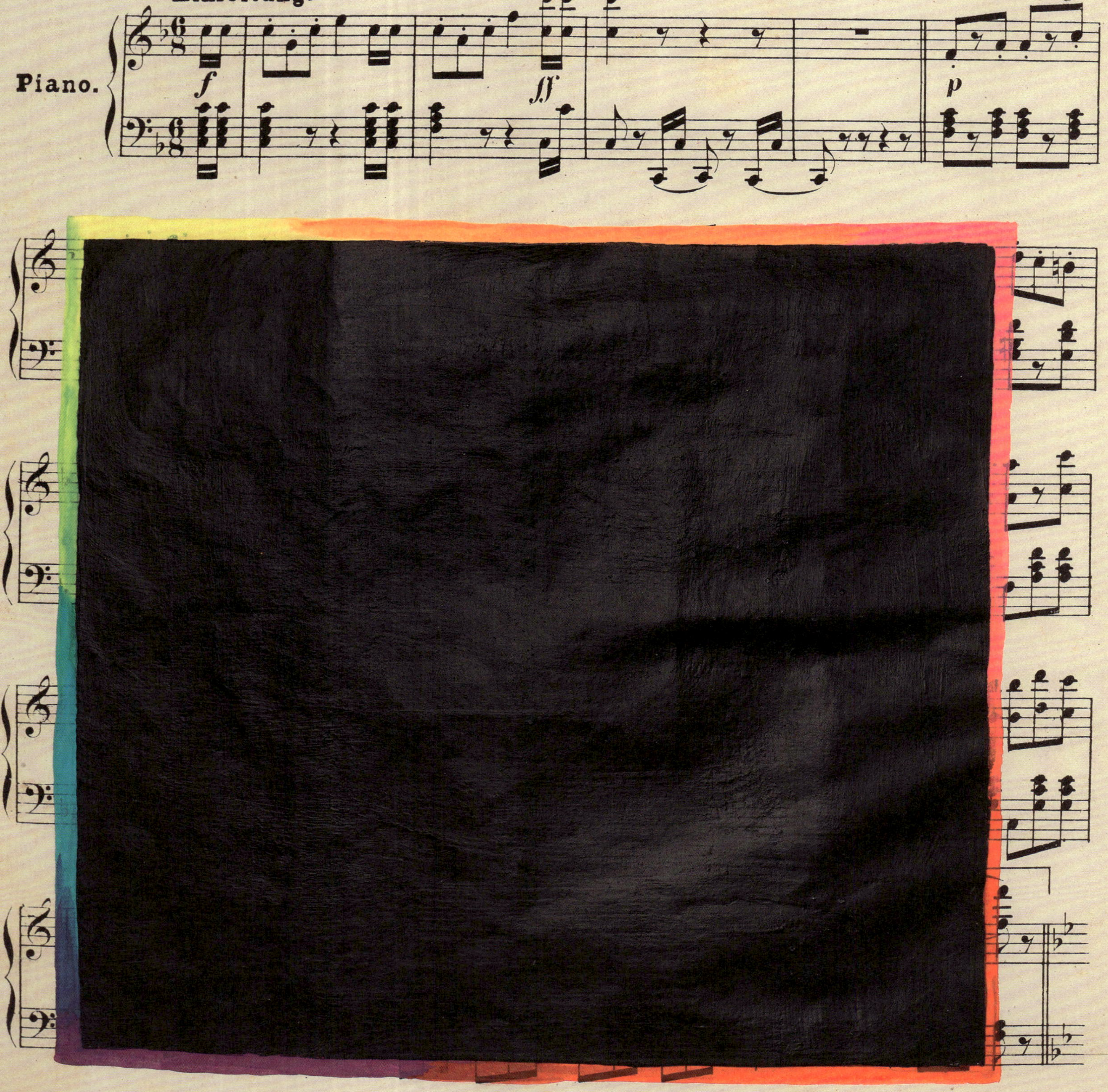

L. M. 436

Stich und Schnellpressendruck der Röder'schen Officin in Leipzig.

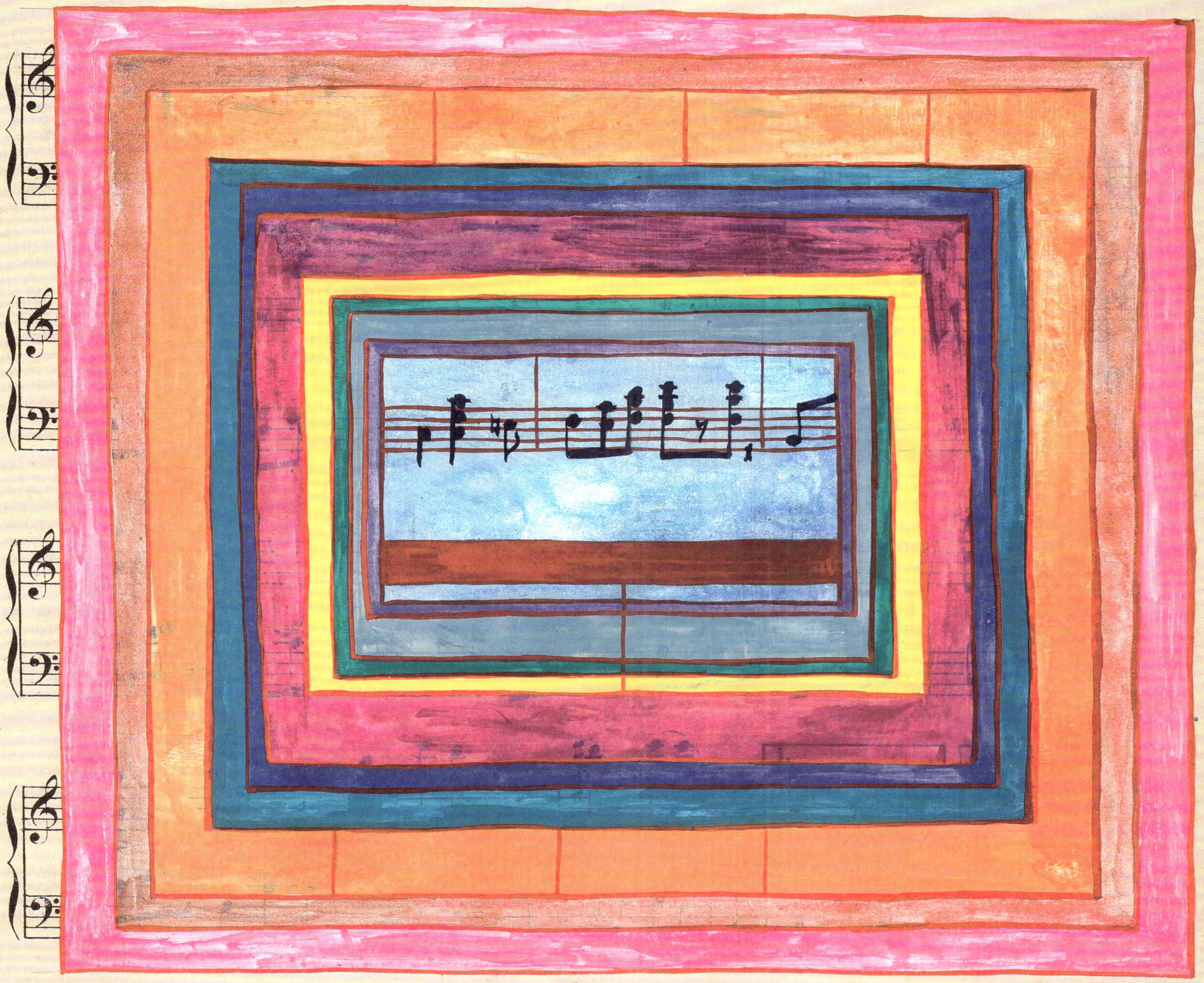

Finale.

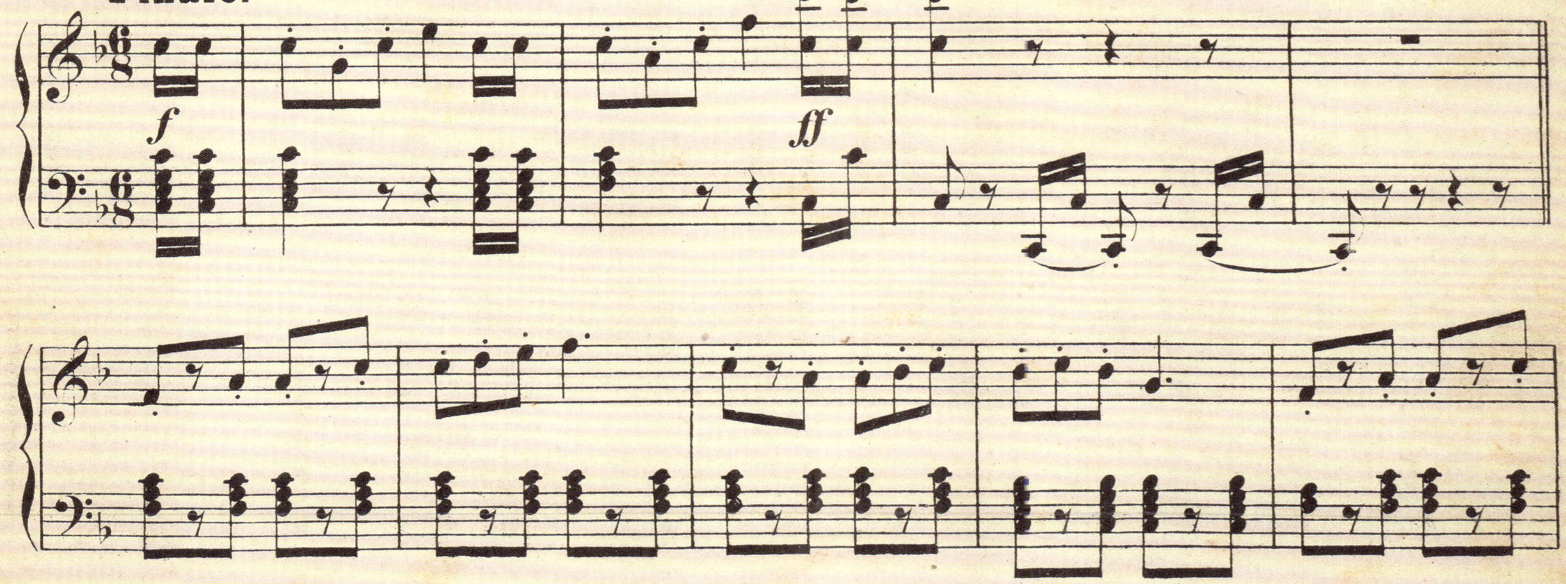

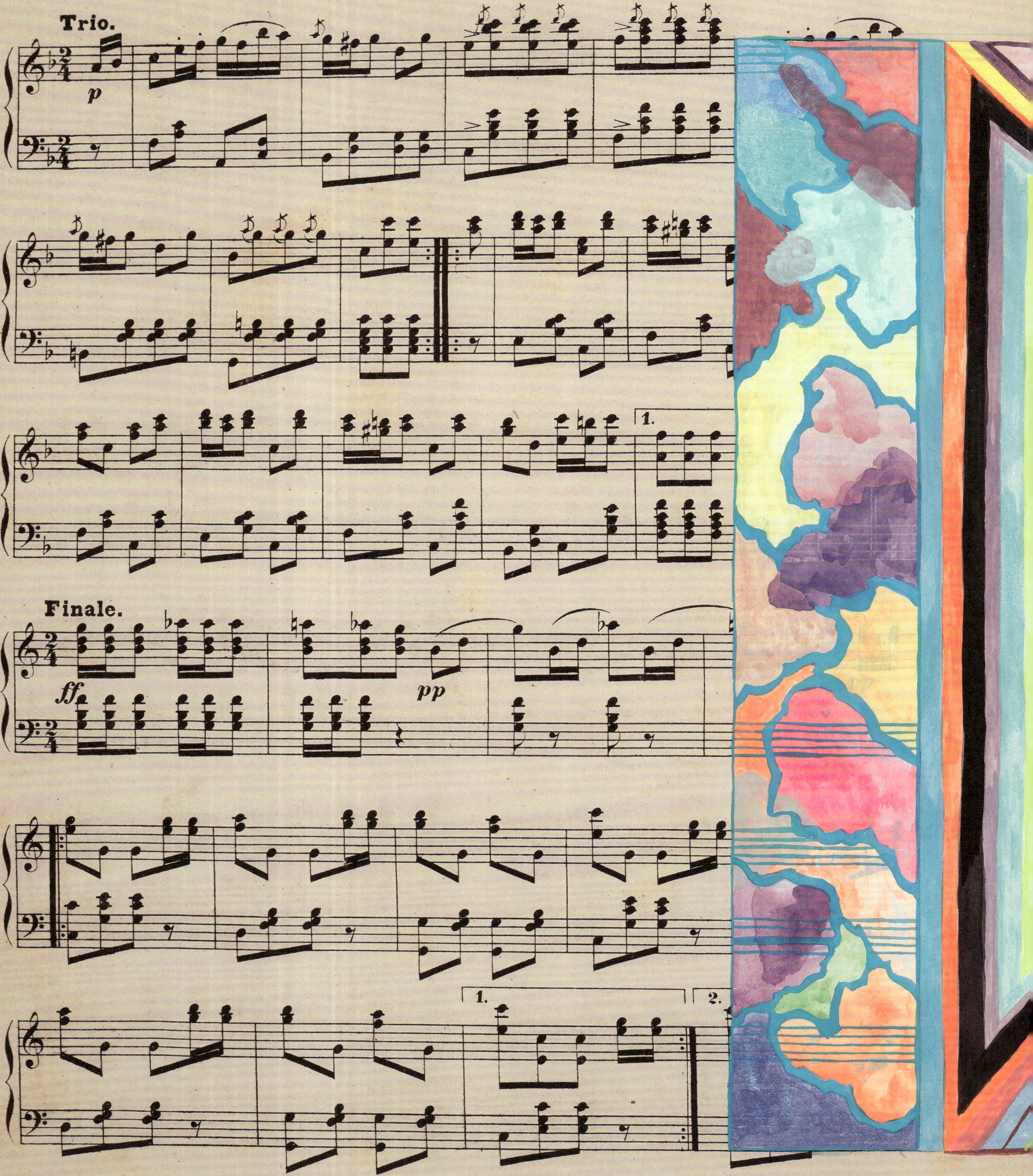
Trio.
p
1.
Finale.
ff
pp
1.
2.

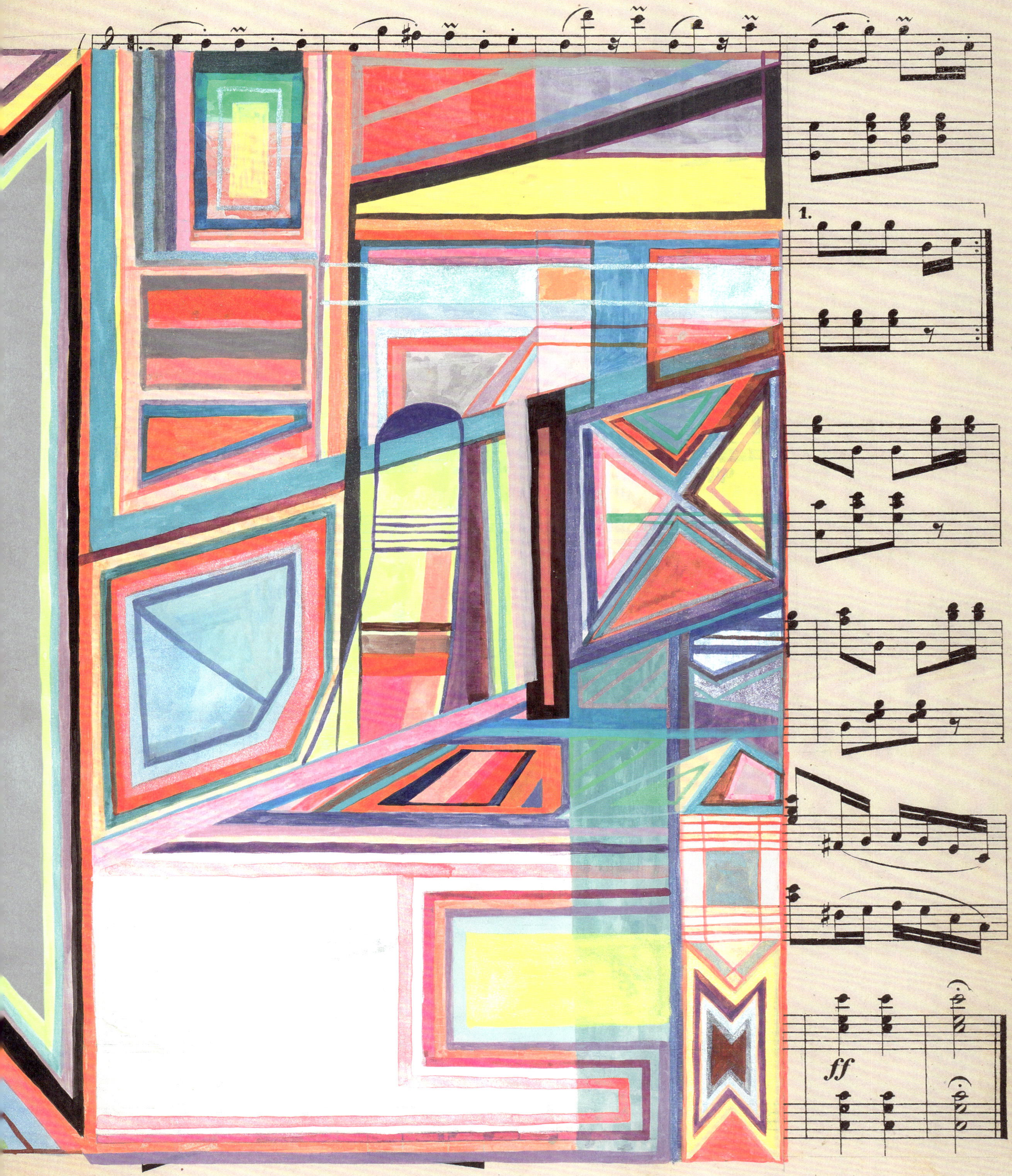
1.
ff

Coda.

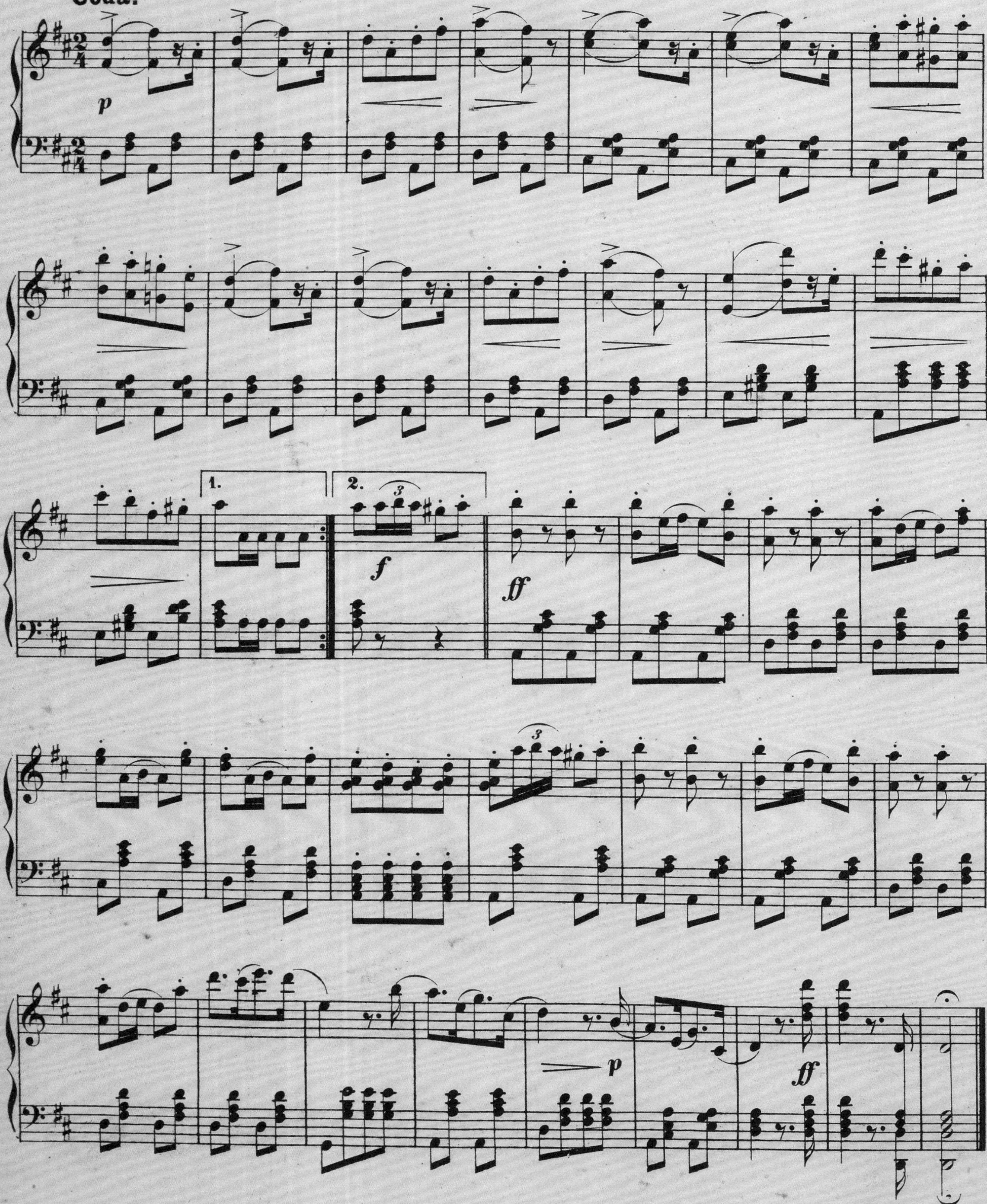

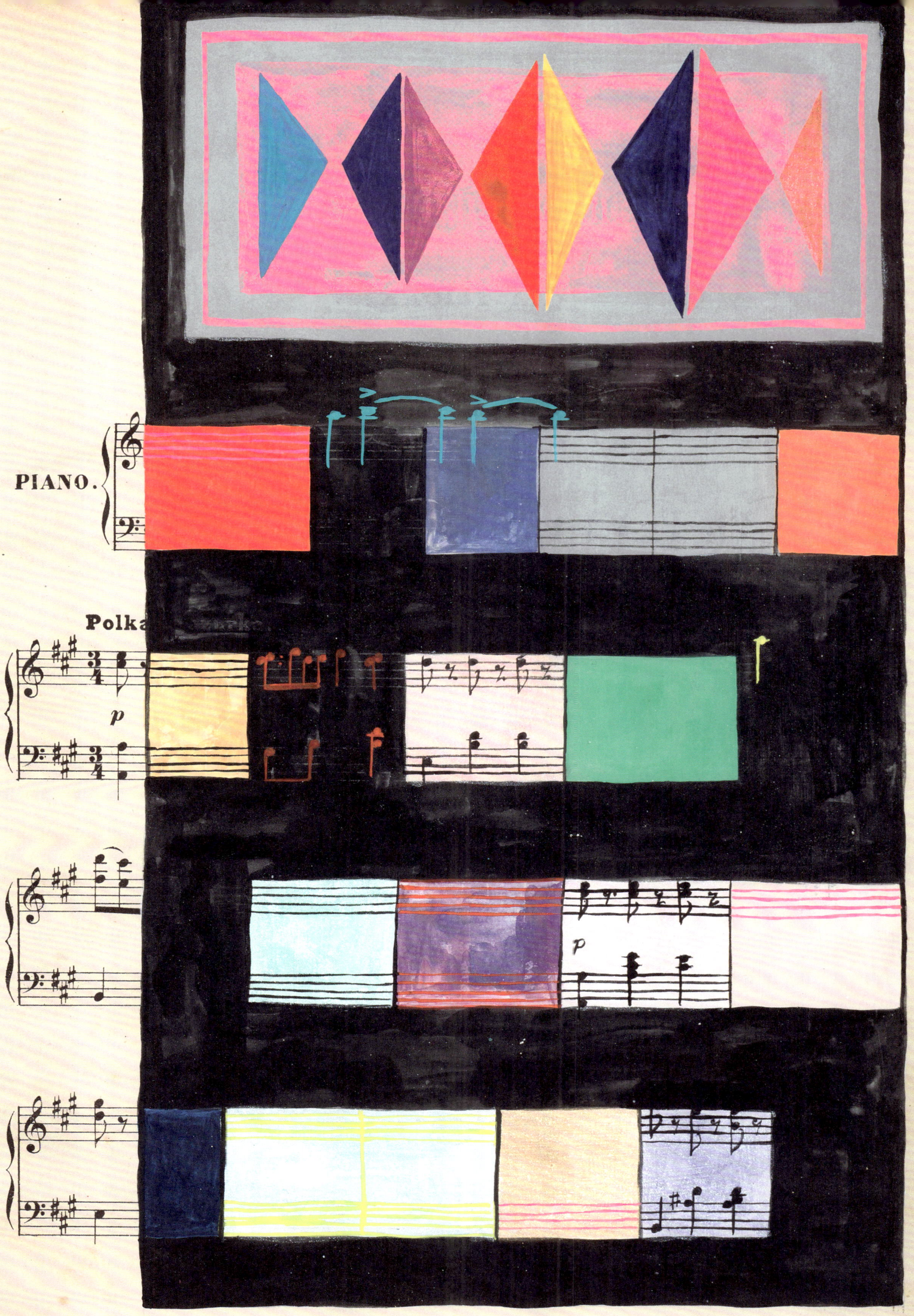
PIANO.
Polka
p
p

Nº 3.

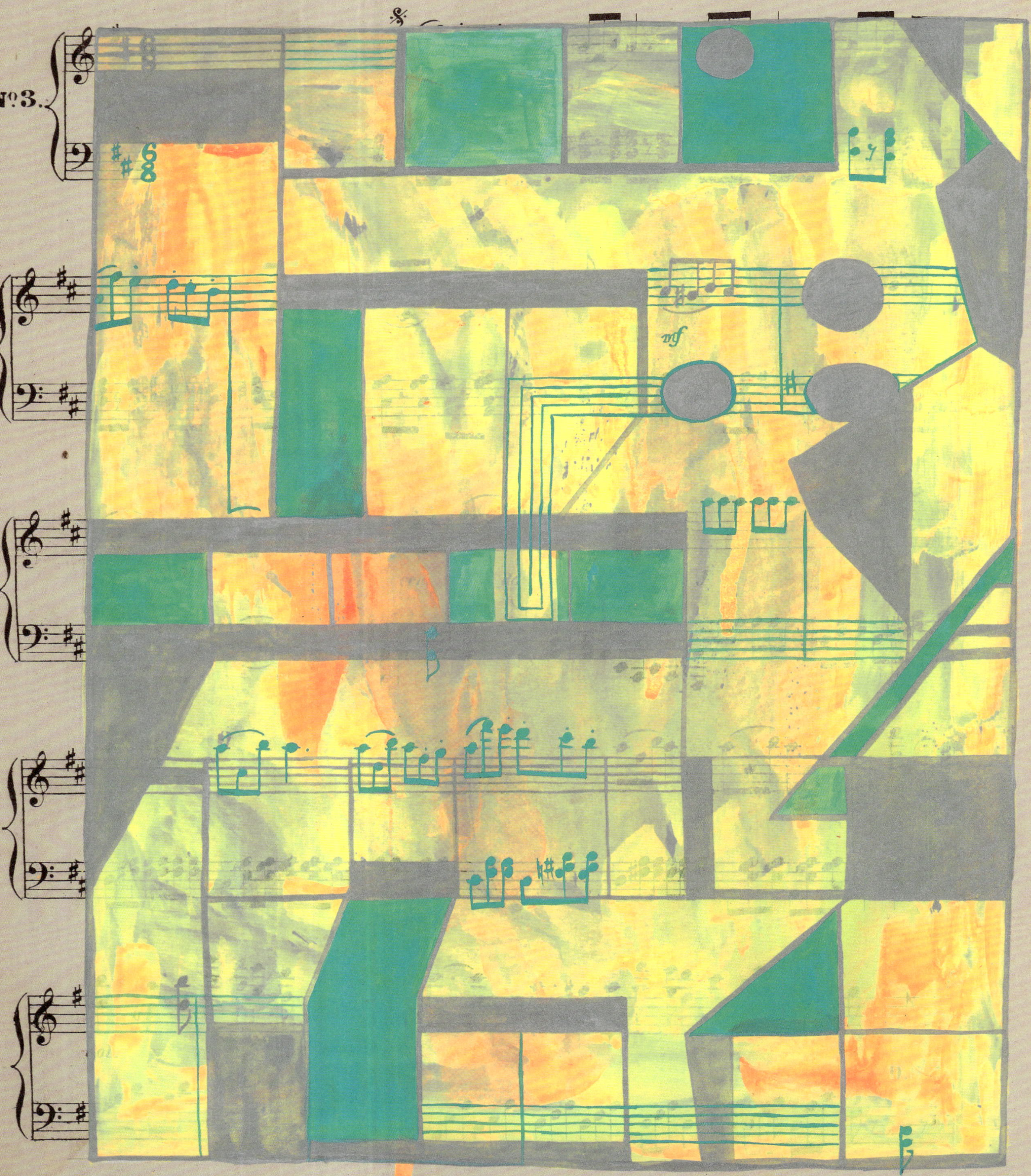

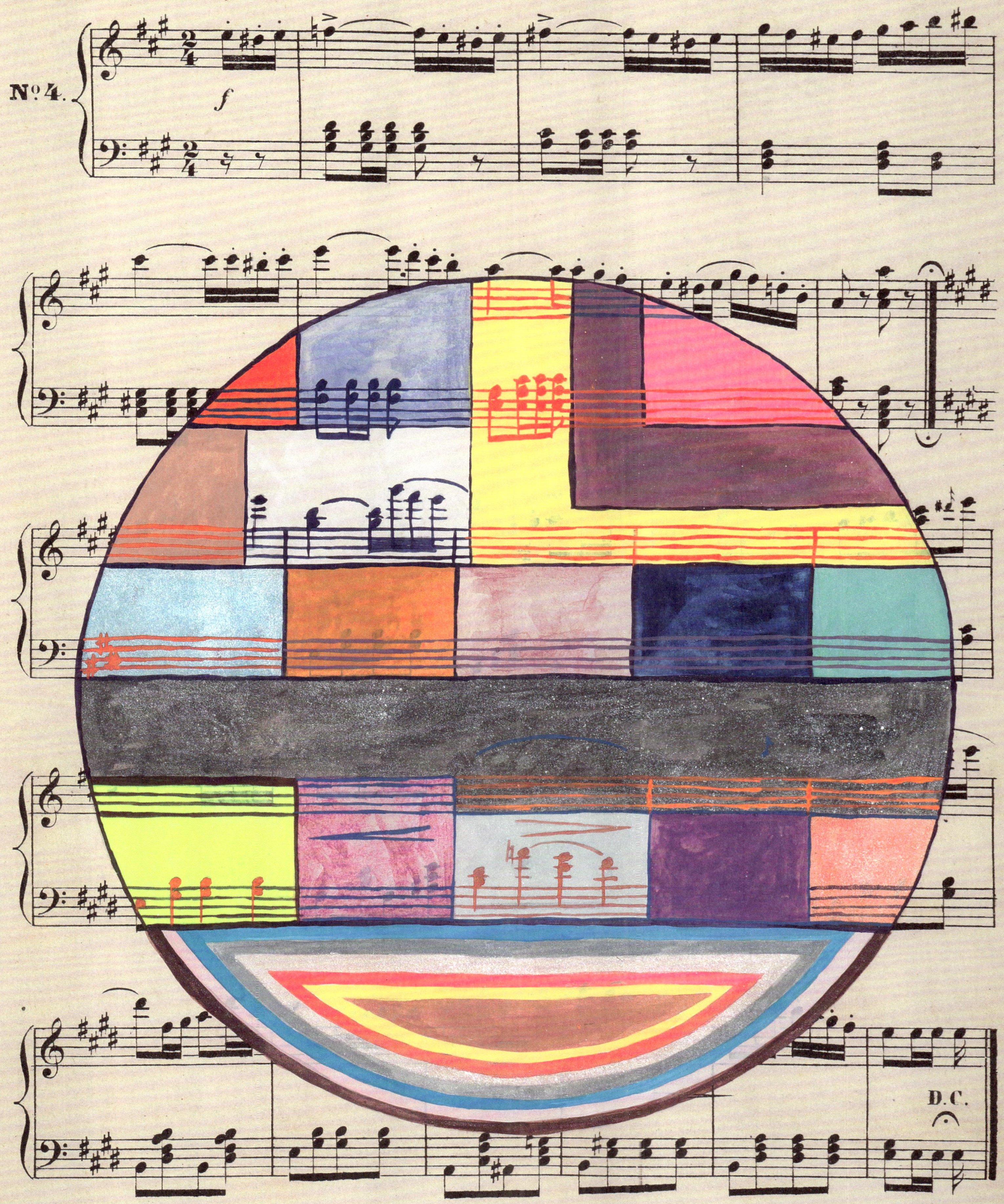
Nº 4.
f
D.C.

No 5.

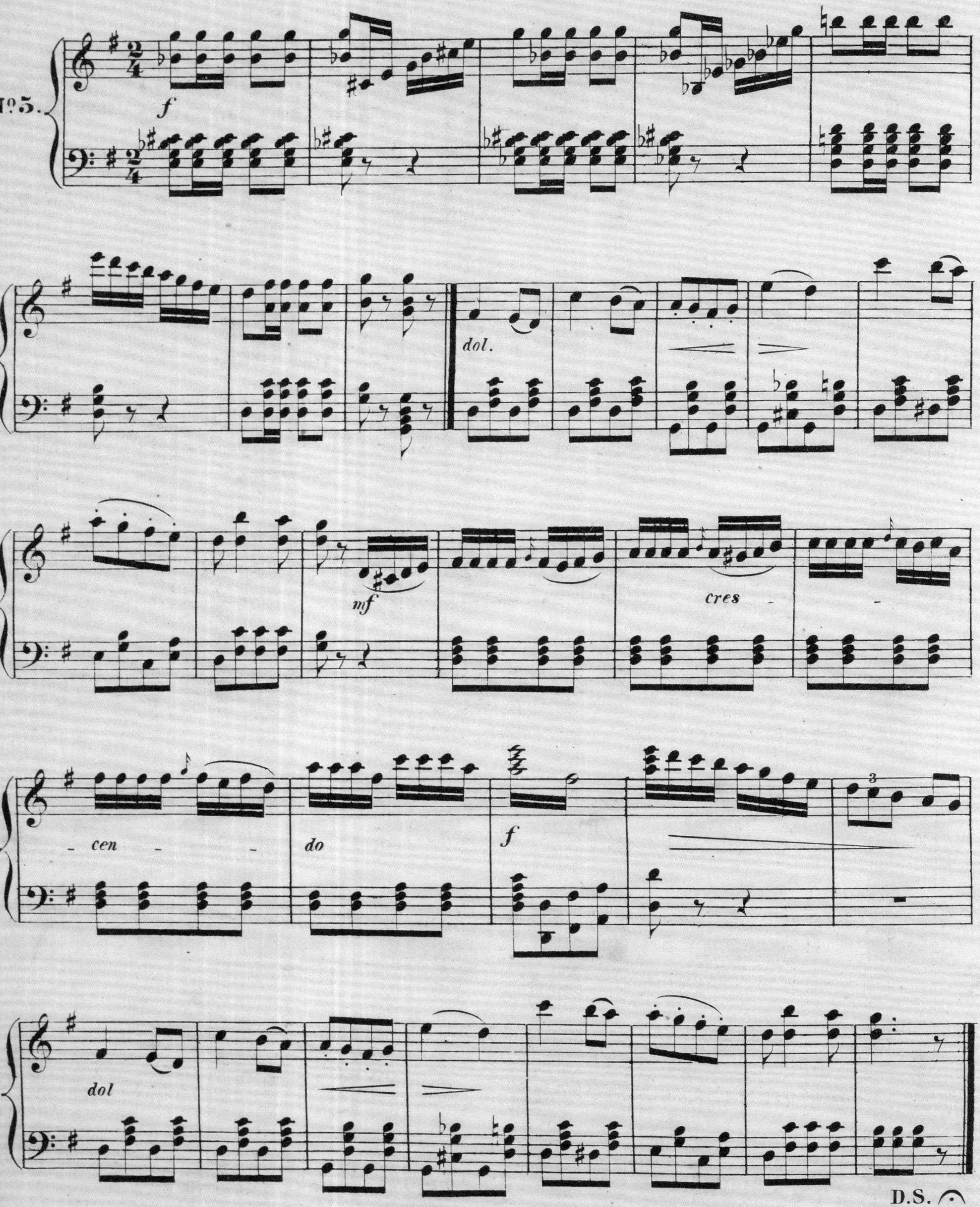

Finale.

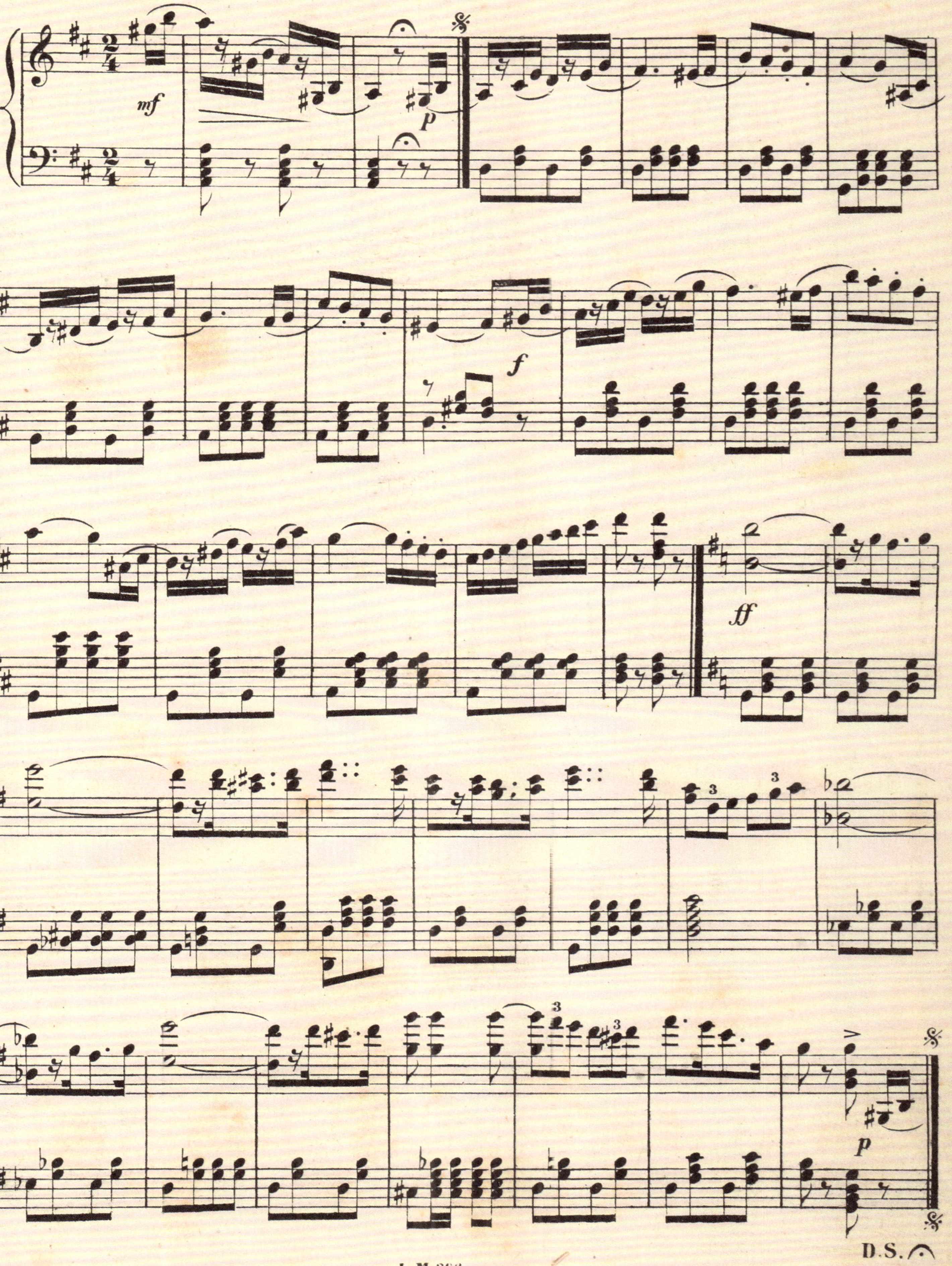

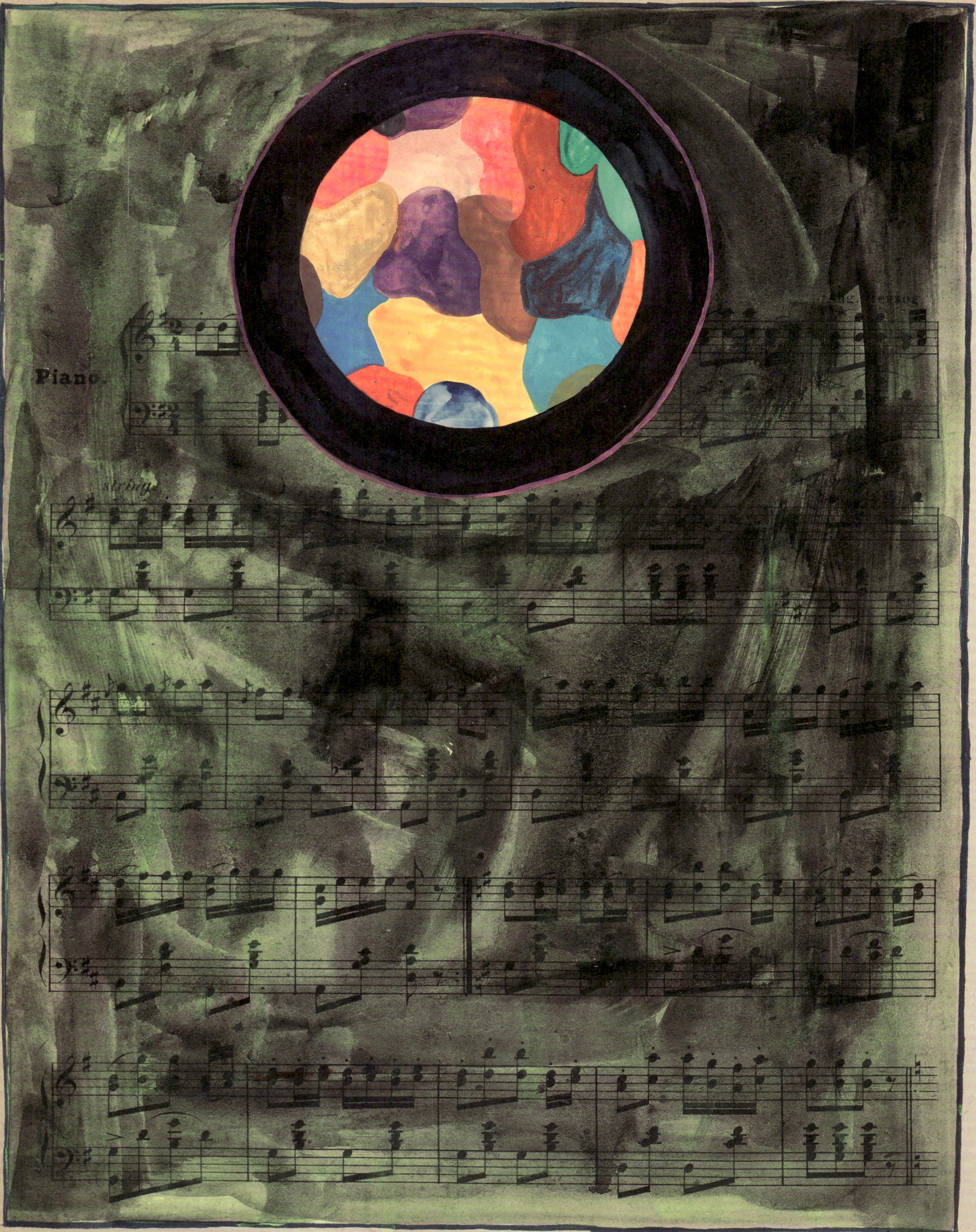
Piano.

4

Trio.

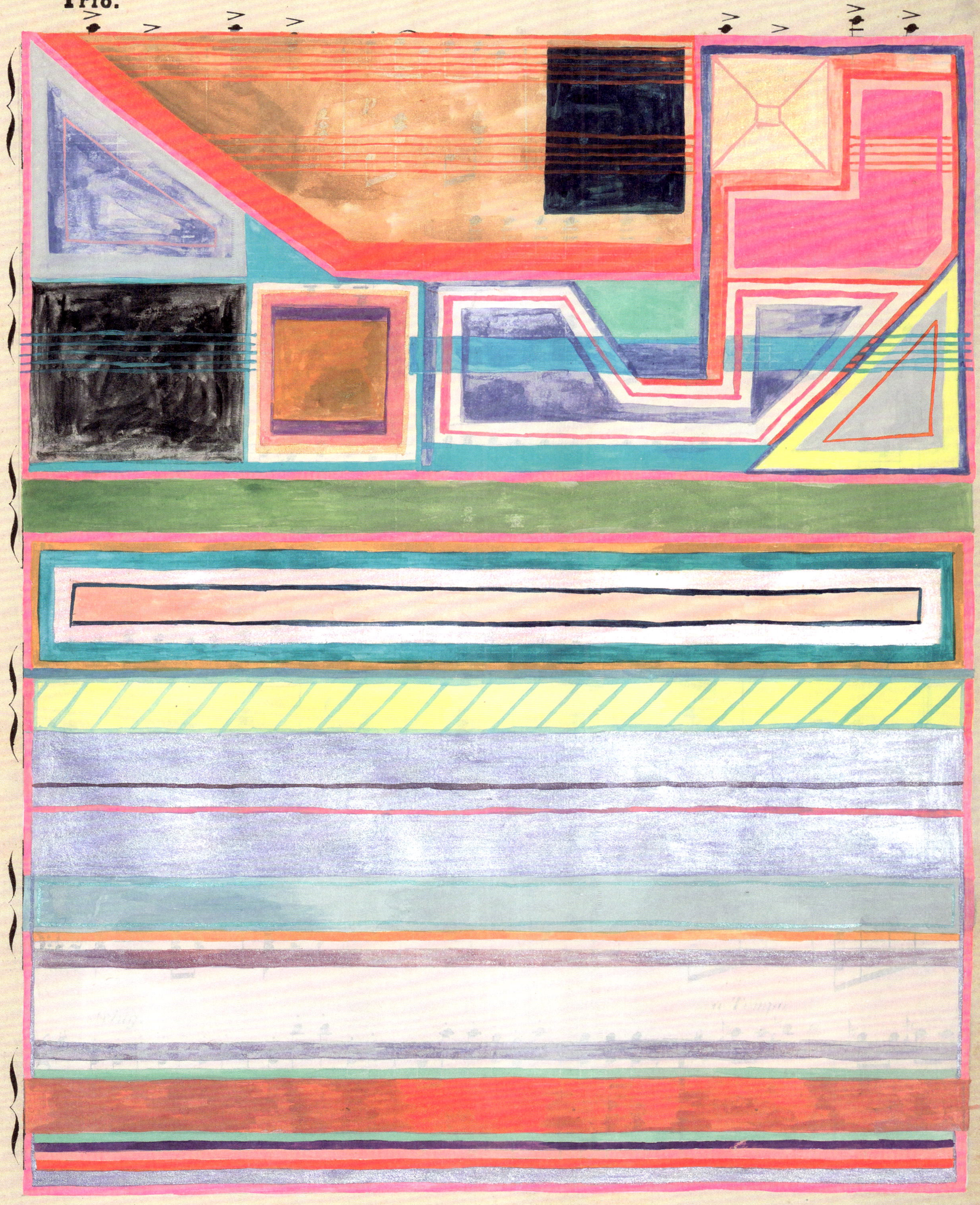

FINALE.

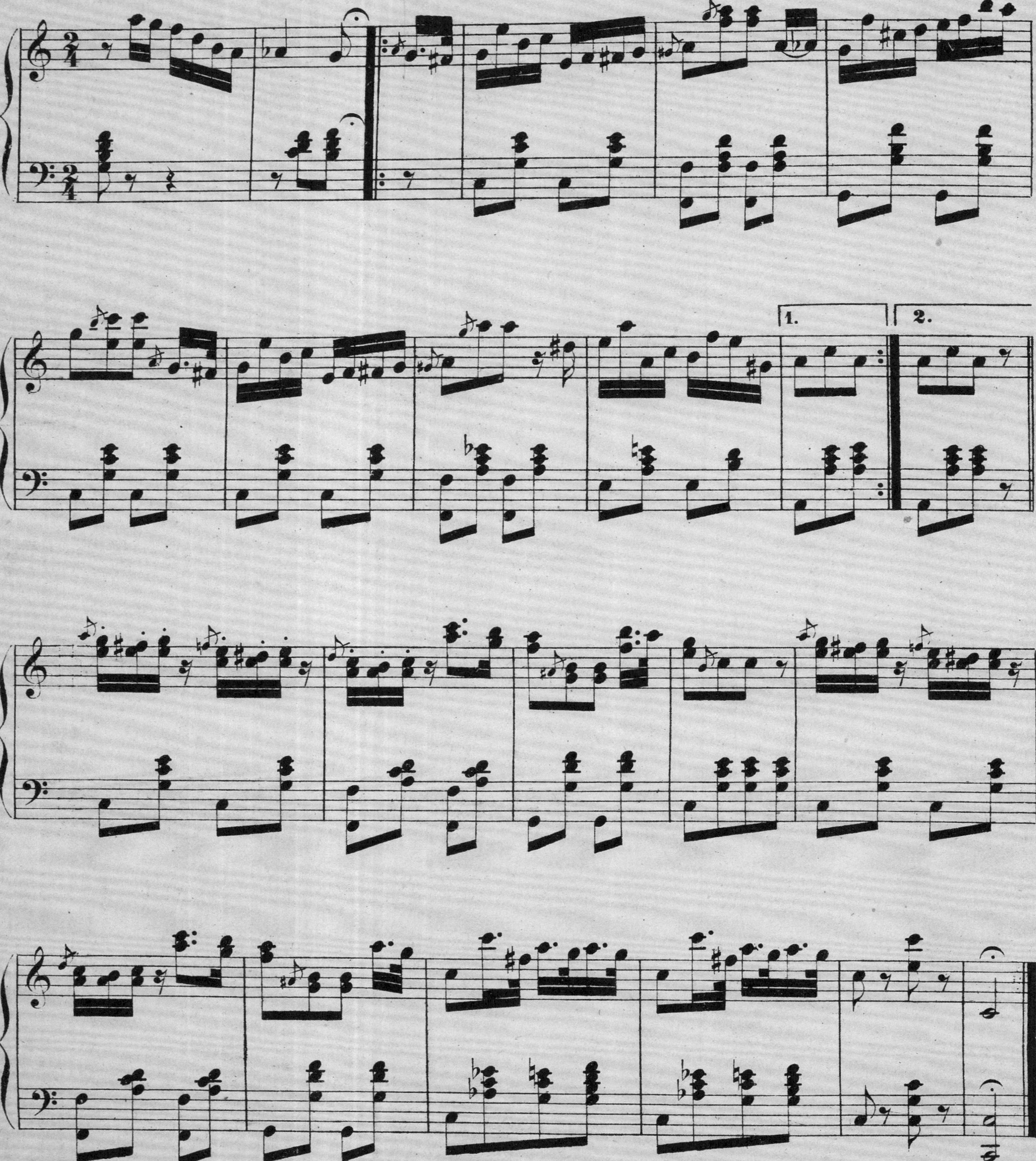

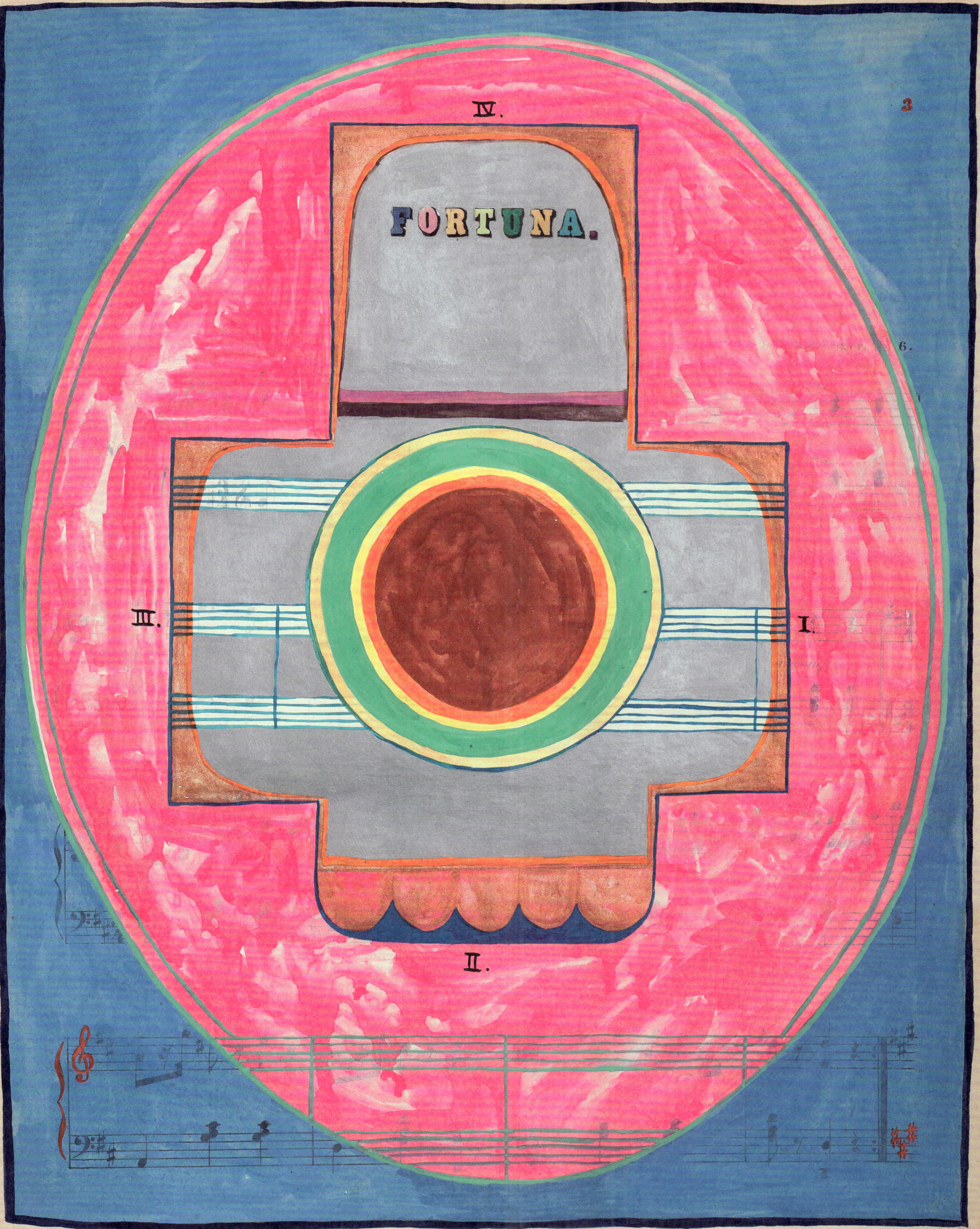
IV.
FORTUNA.
III.
I.
II.

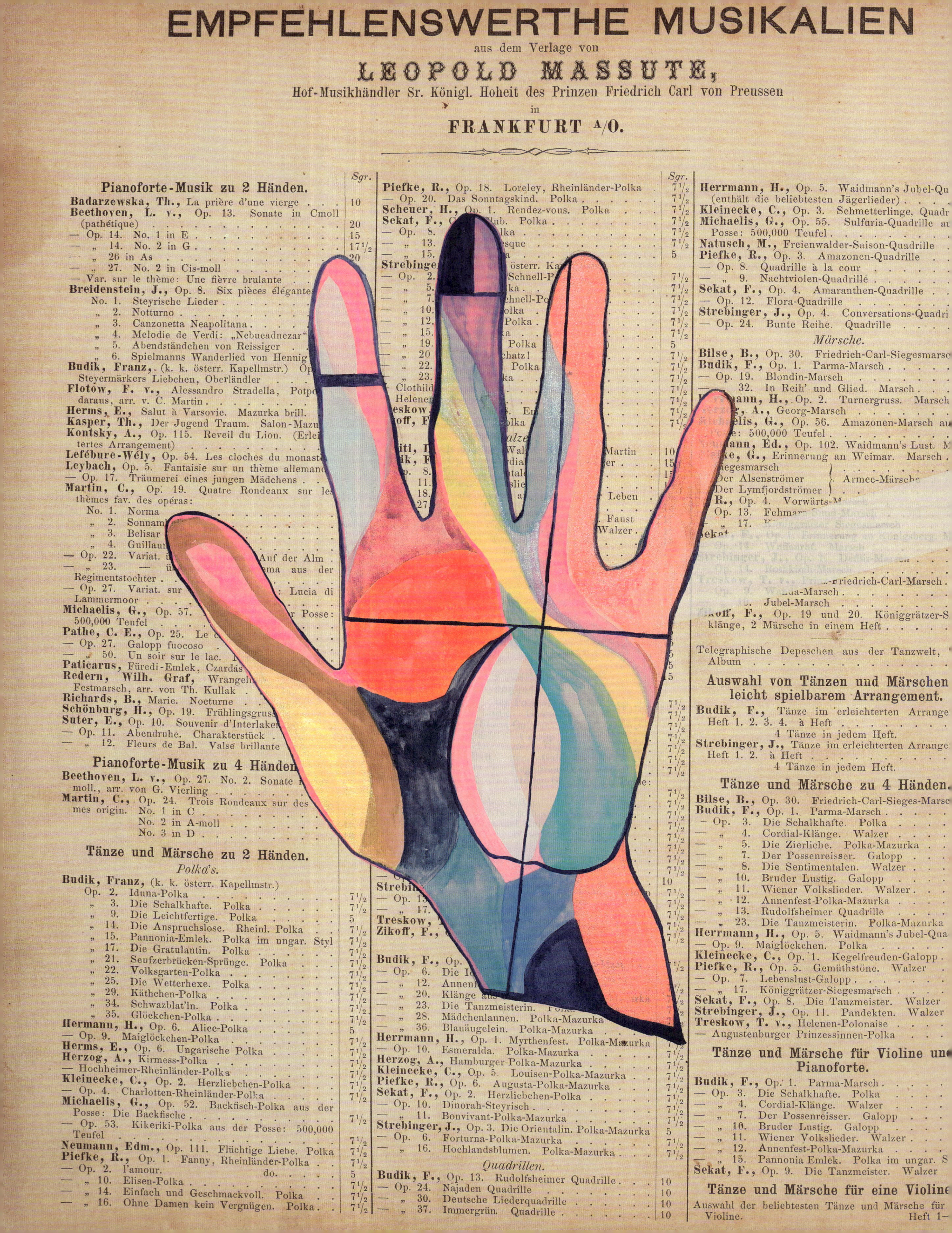
EMPFEHLENSWERTHE MUSIKALIEN
aus dem Verlage von
LEOPOLD MASSUTE,
Hof-Musikhändler Sr. Königl. Hoheit des Prinzen Friedrich Carl von Preussen
in
FRANKFURT A/O.
Pianoforte-Musik zu 2 Händen.
Pianoforte-Musik zu 4 Händen.
Tänze und Märsche zu 2 Händen.
Polka's.
Quadrillen.
Märsche.
Auswahl von Tänzen und Märschen leicht spielbarem Arrangement.
Tänze und Märsche zu 4 Händen.
Tänze und Märsche für Violine und Pianoforte.
Tänze und Märsche für eine Violine

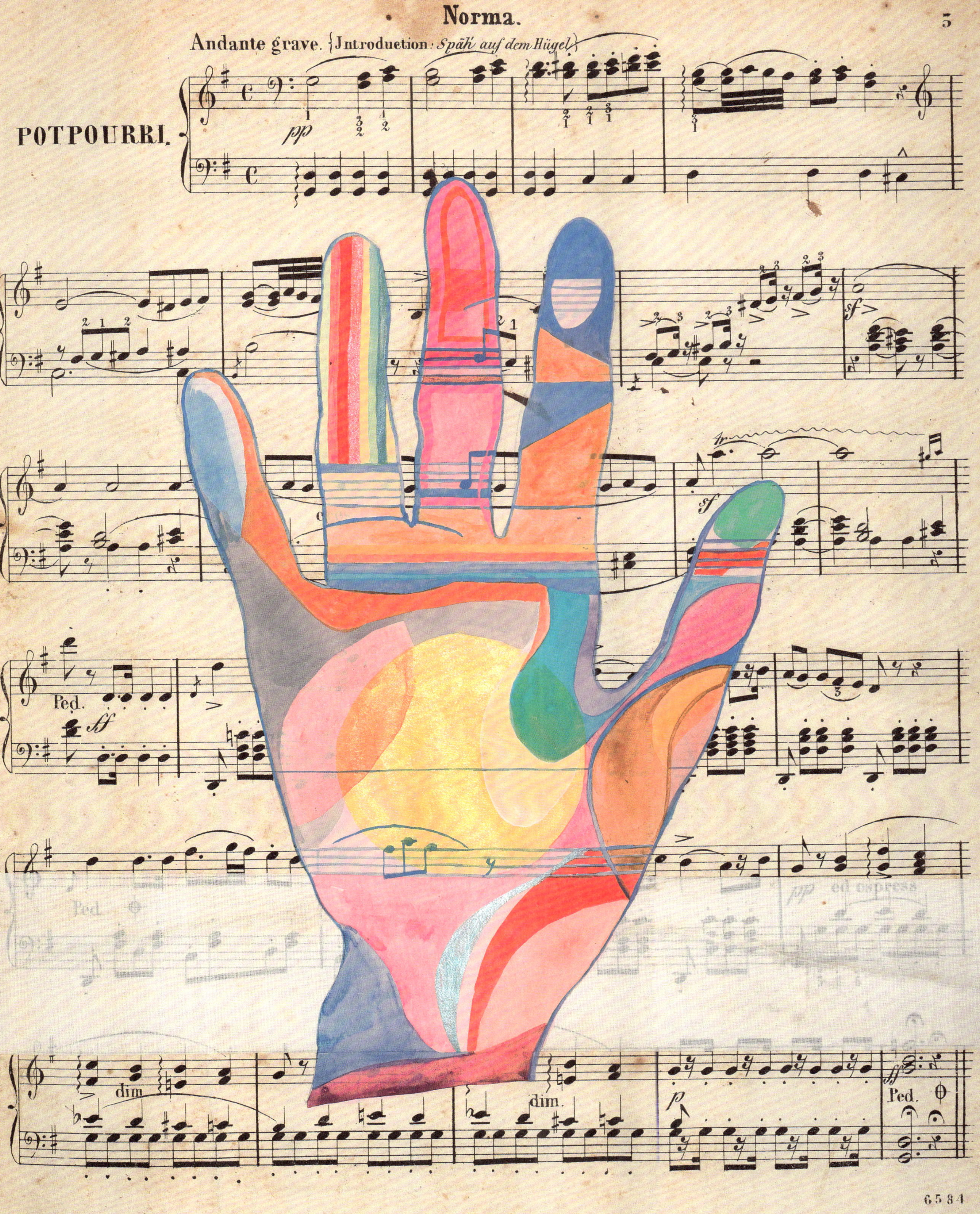
Norma.
3
Andante grave. {Jntroduction: Spăh auf dem Hügel}
POTPOURRI.
pp
sf
Ped.
ff
ed espress
dim
dim.
p
Ped.
6584

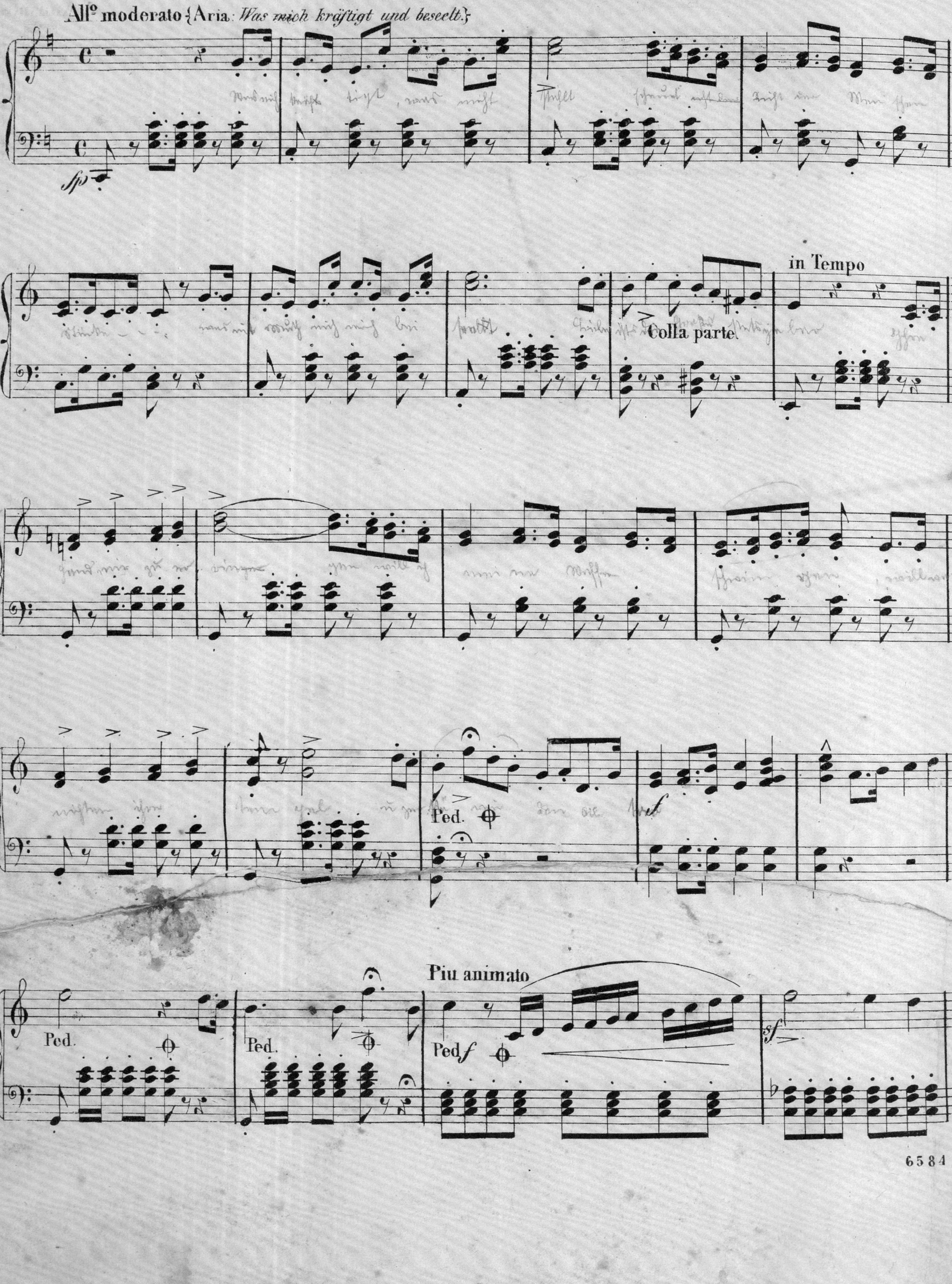
All° moderato {Aria: Was mich kräftigt und beseelt.}
in Tempo
Colla parte
Ped.
Piu animato
Ped
f
sf

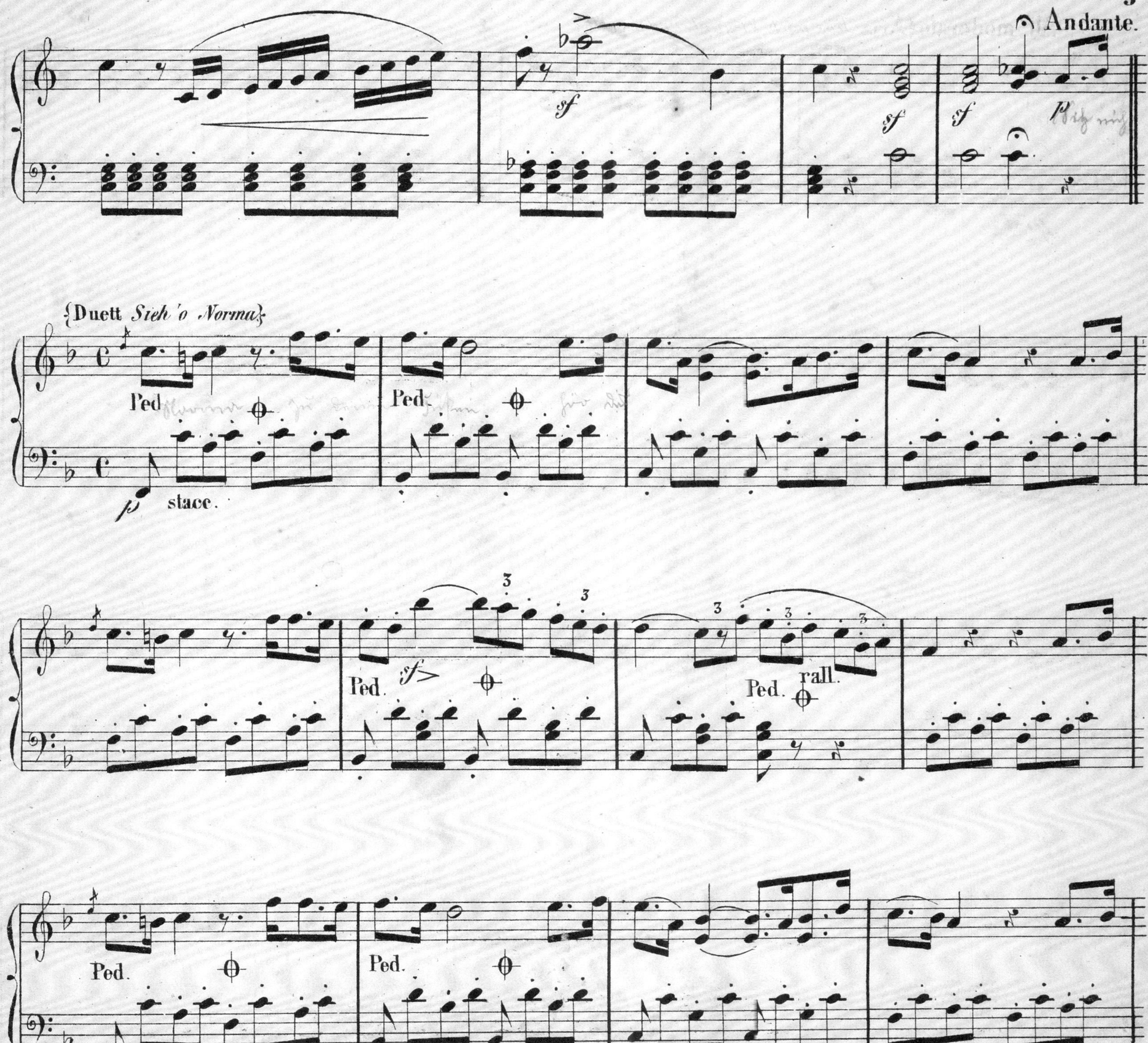
Andante.
sf
Duett Sieh' o Norma
Ped
p
stacc.
rall.
Ped.
sf
p

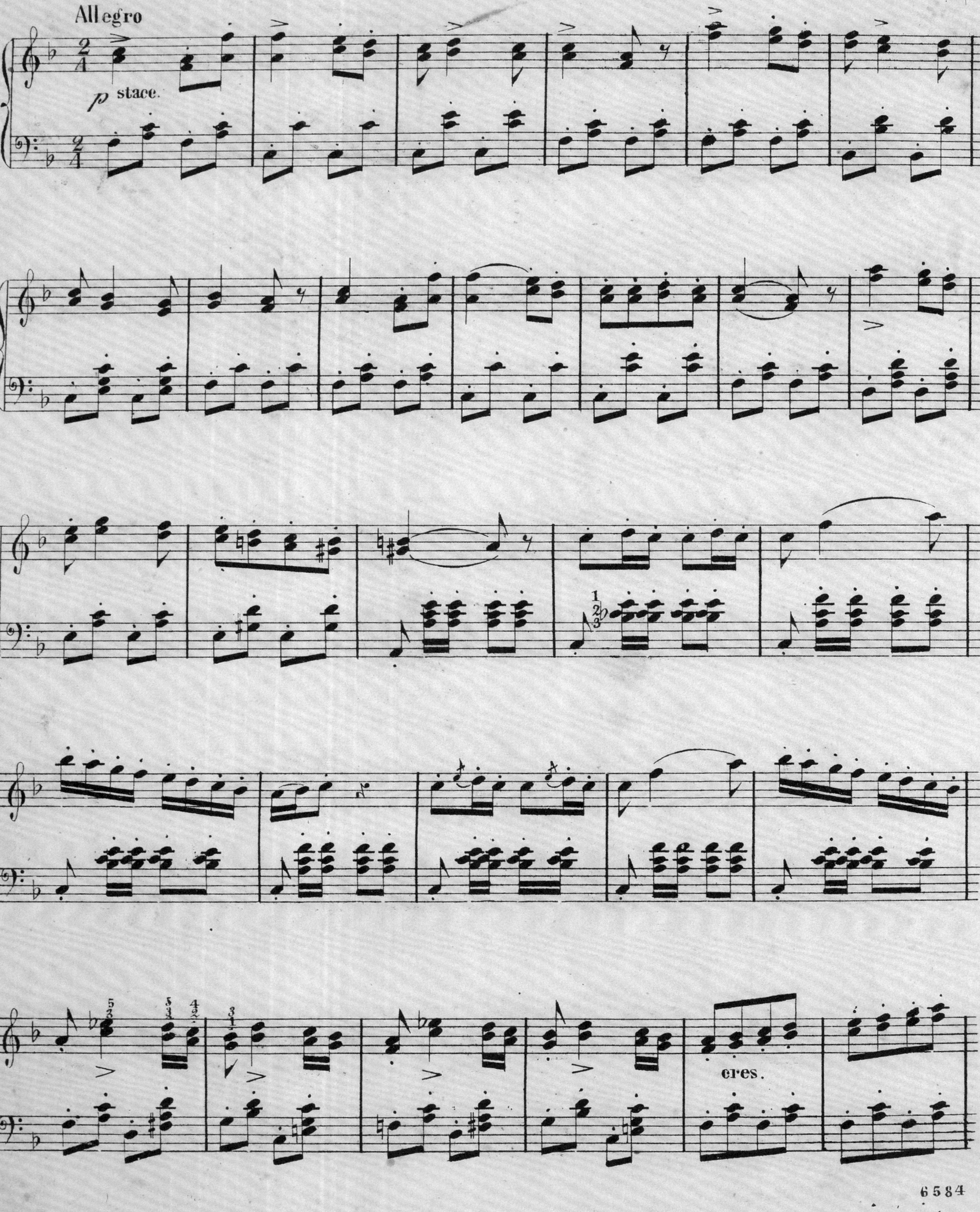
Allegro
p stacc.
cres.

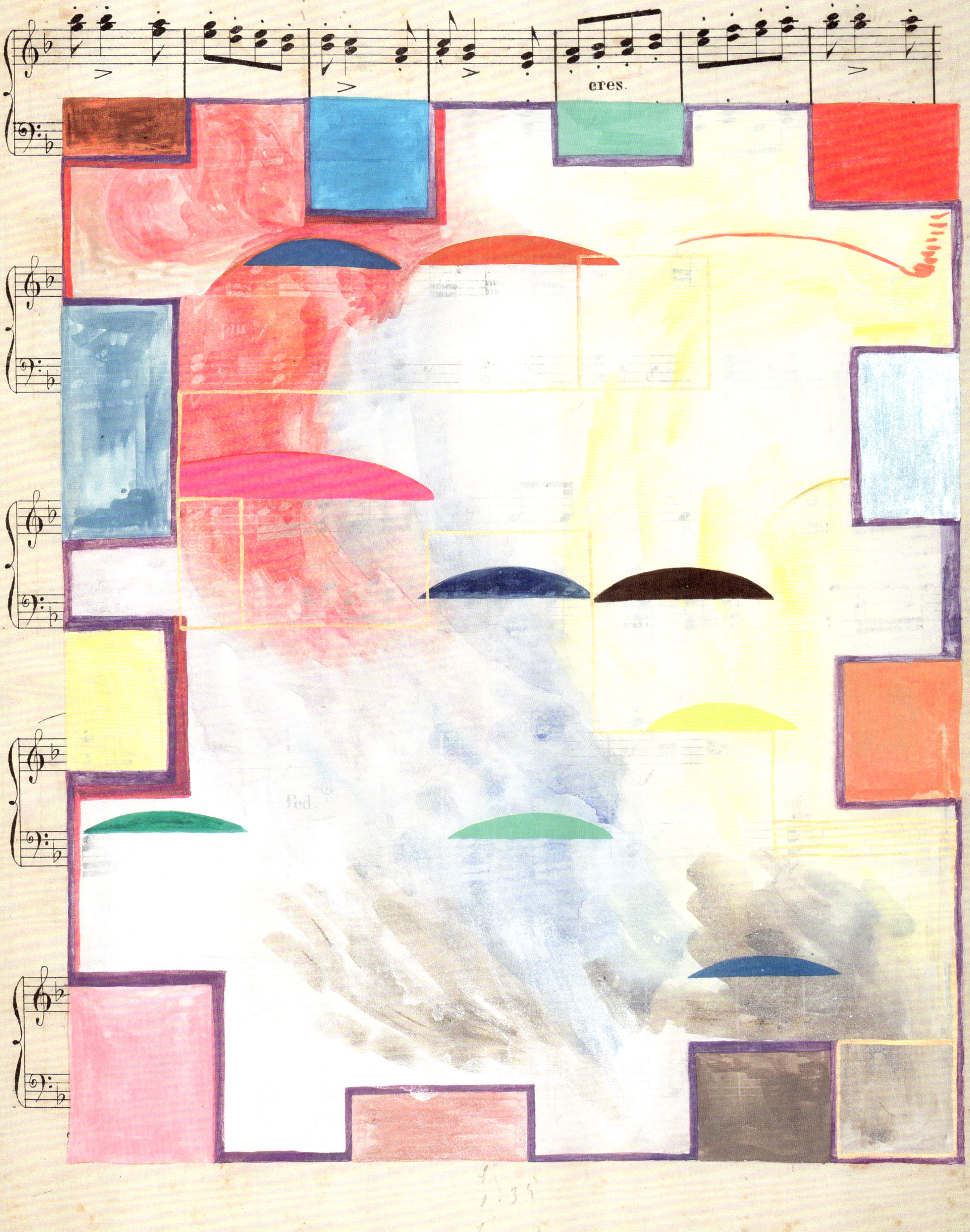
cres.
Ped

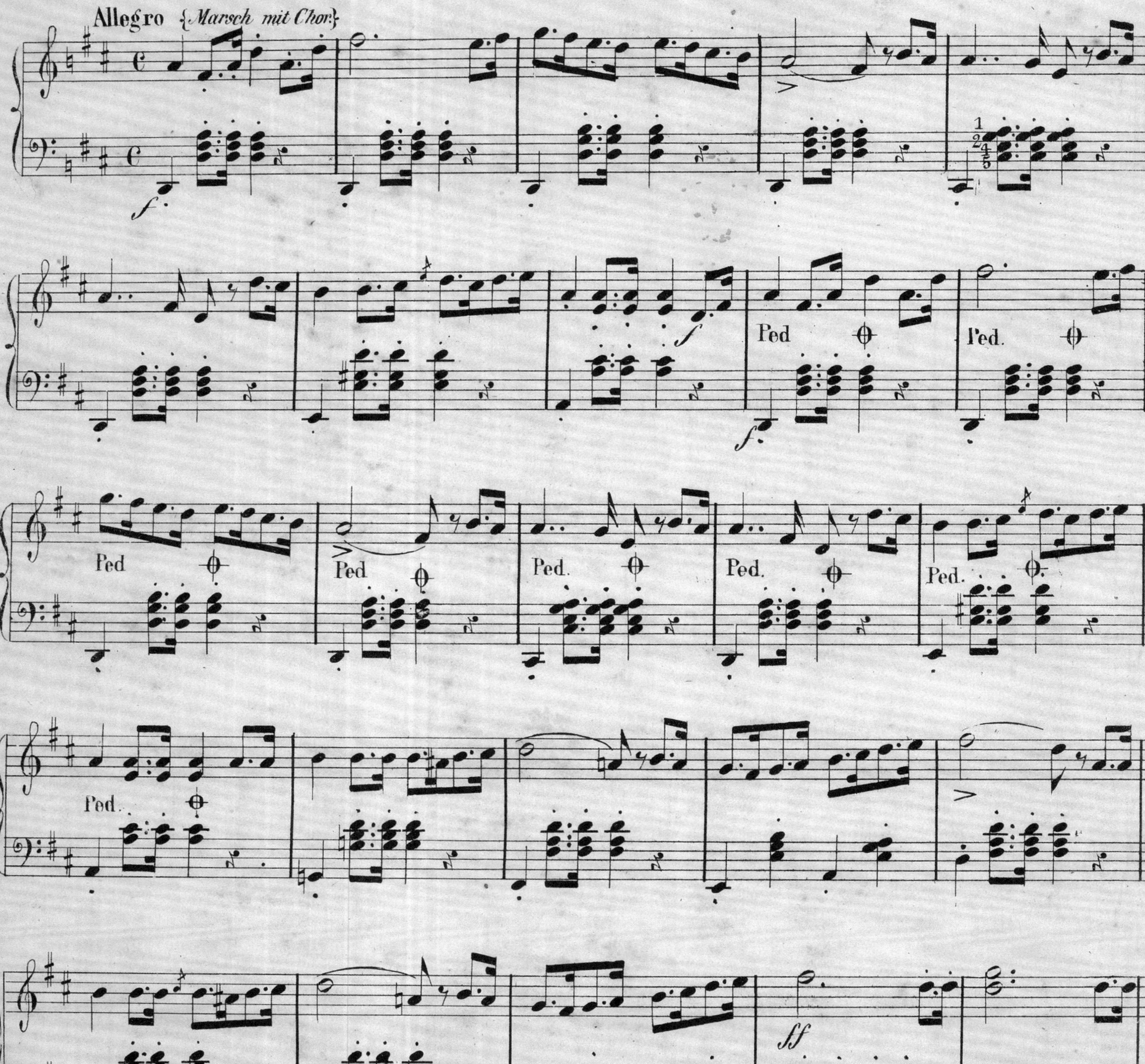
Allegro {Marsch mit Chor}
Ped.
ff
sf

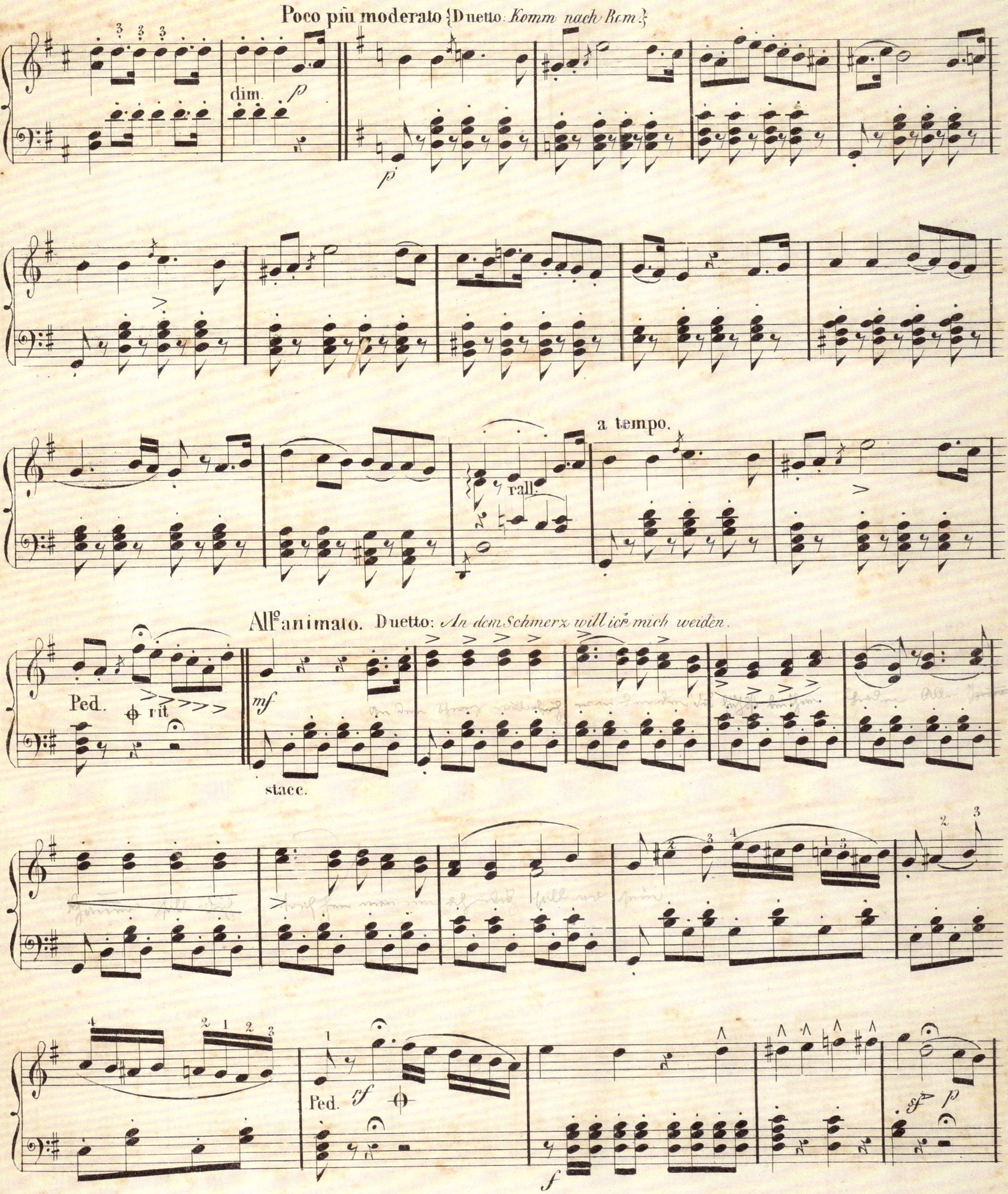
Poco più moderato {Duetto: Komm nach Rom.}
dim.
rall.
a tempo.
Allº animato. Duetto: An dem Schmerz will ich mich weiden.
Ped.
rit
stacc.
Ped.

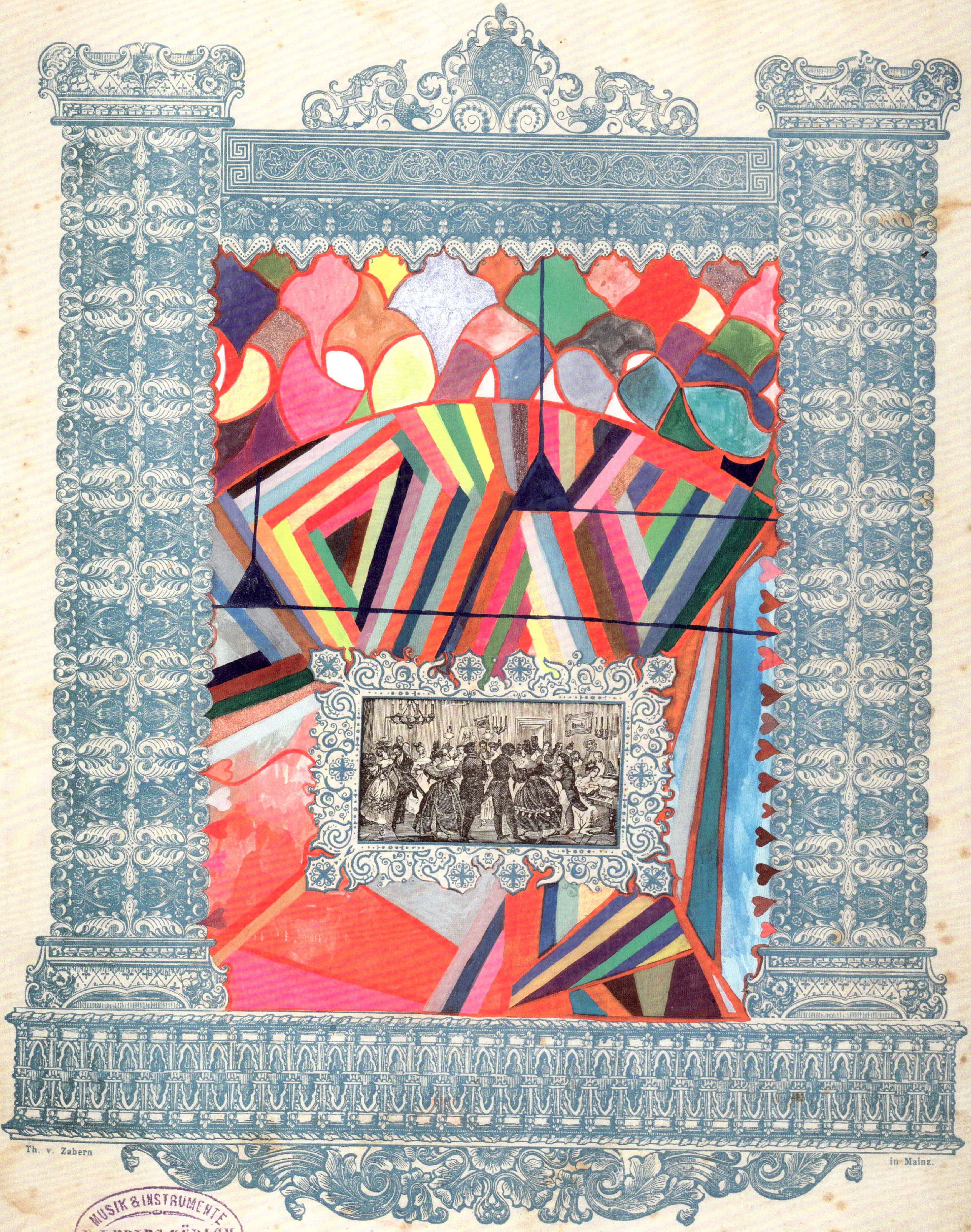
Th. v. Zabern
in Mainz.

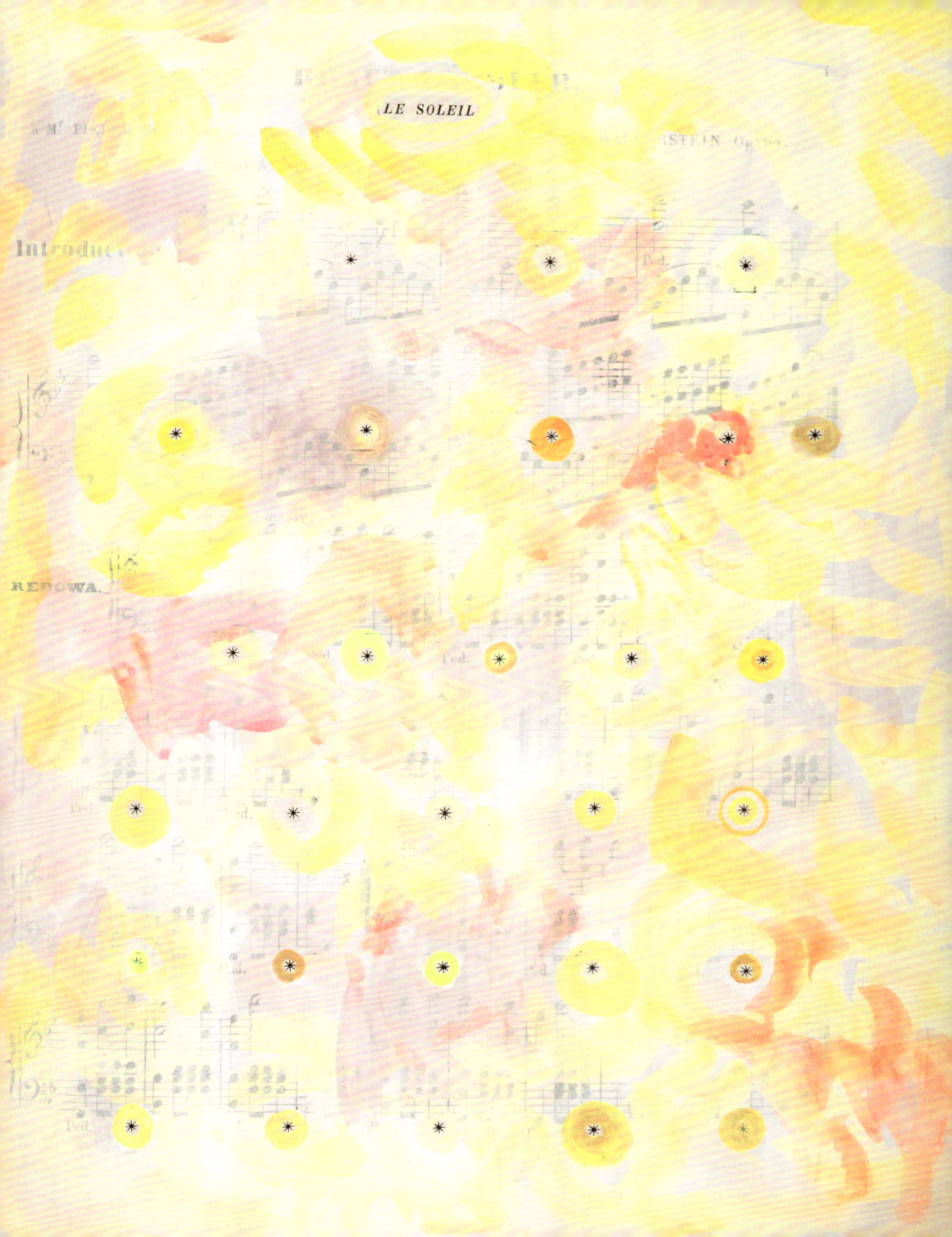
LE SOLEIL
REDOWA.

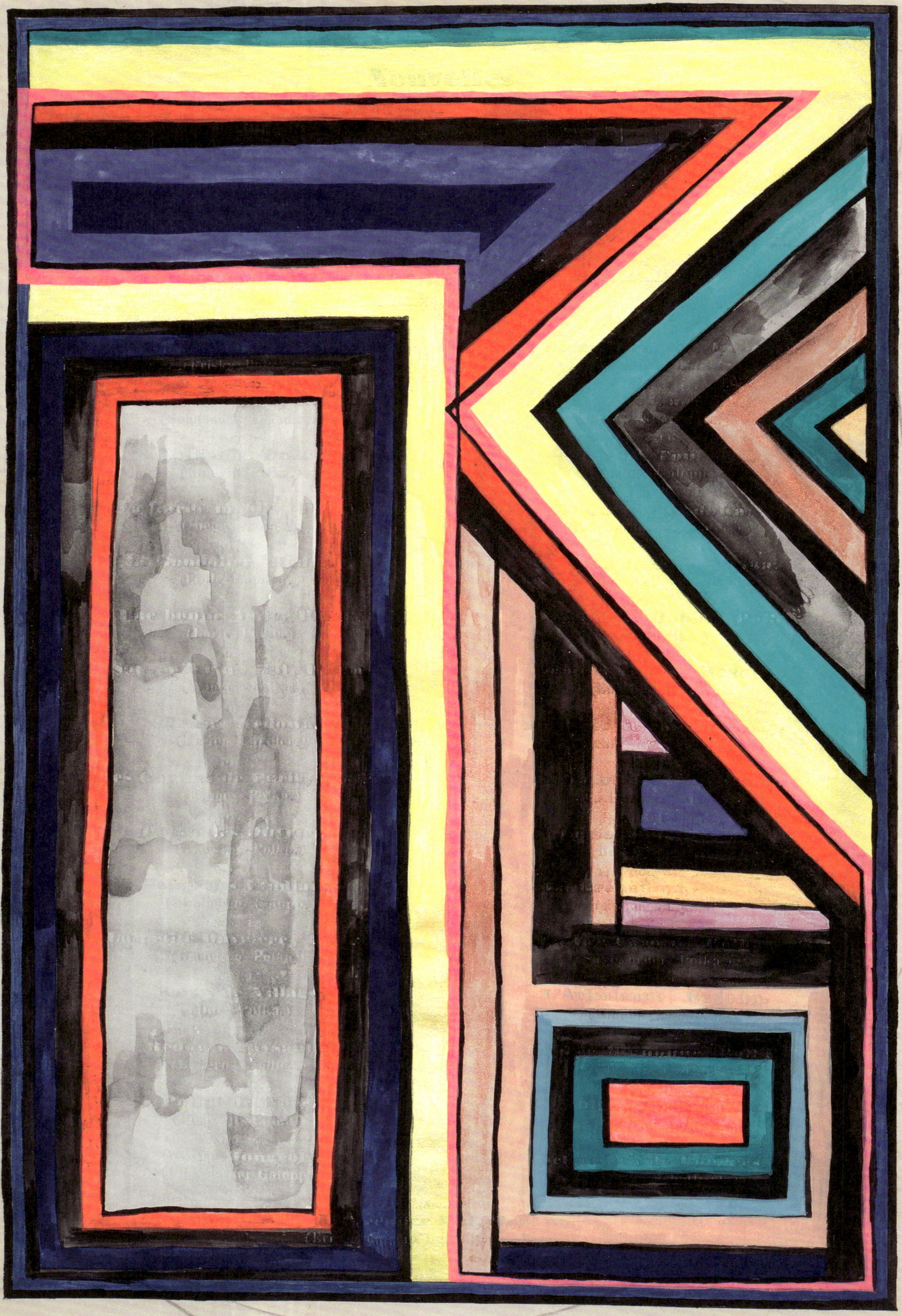

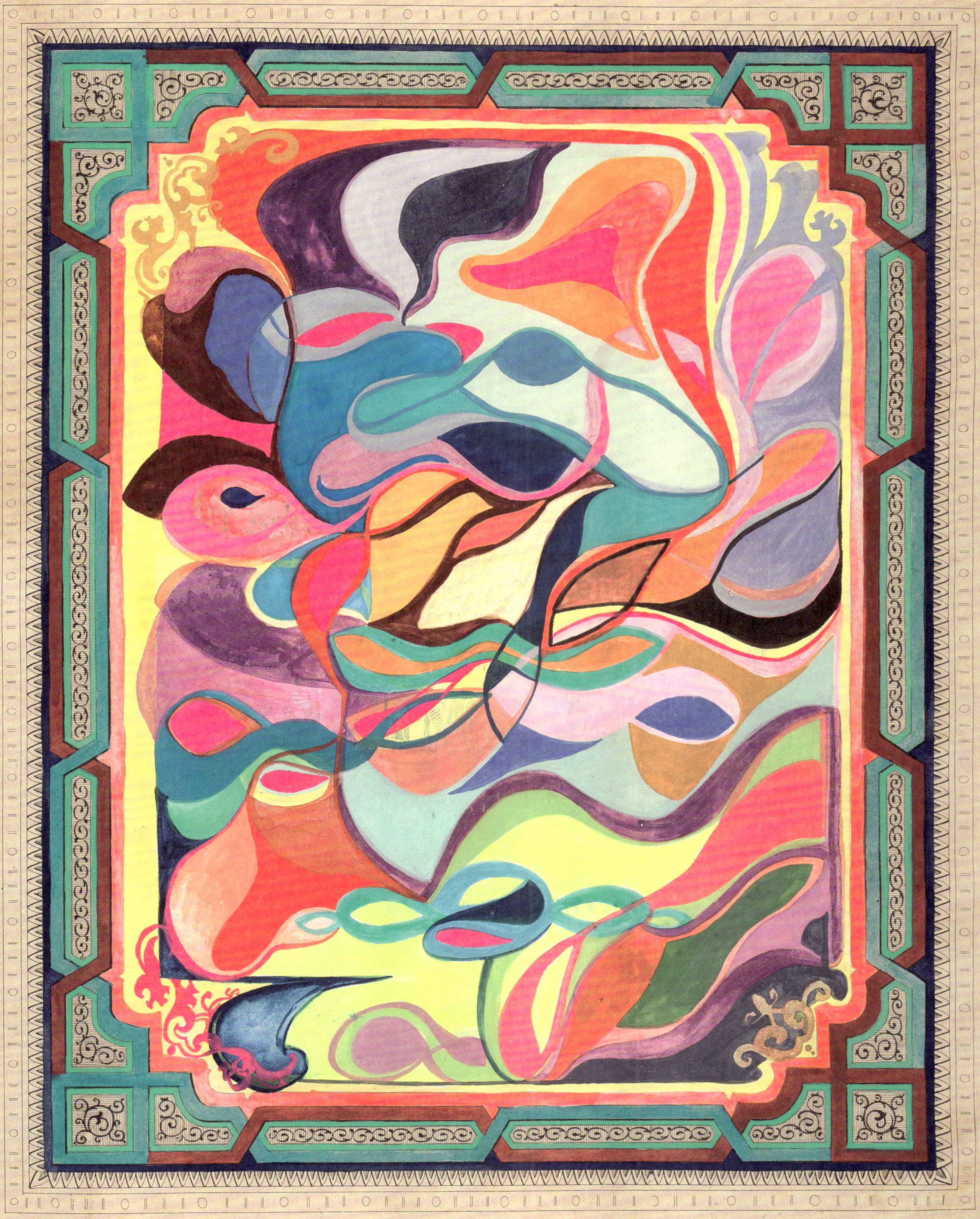

Lith. Anst. C. G. Röder, Leipzig.

Sechs militärische

Soldatenlieder Märsche

für das

Piano Forte

eingerichtet

von

P. Streck.

Op. 178.

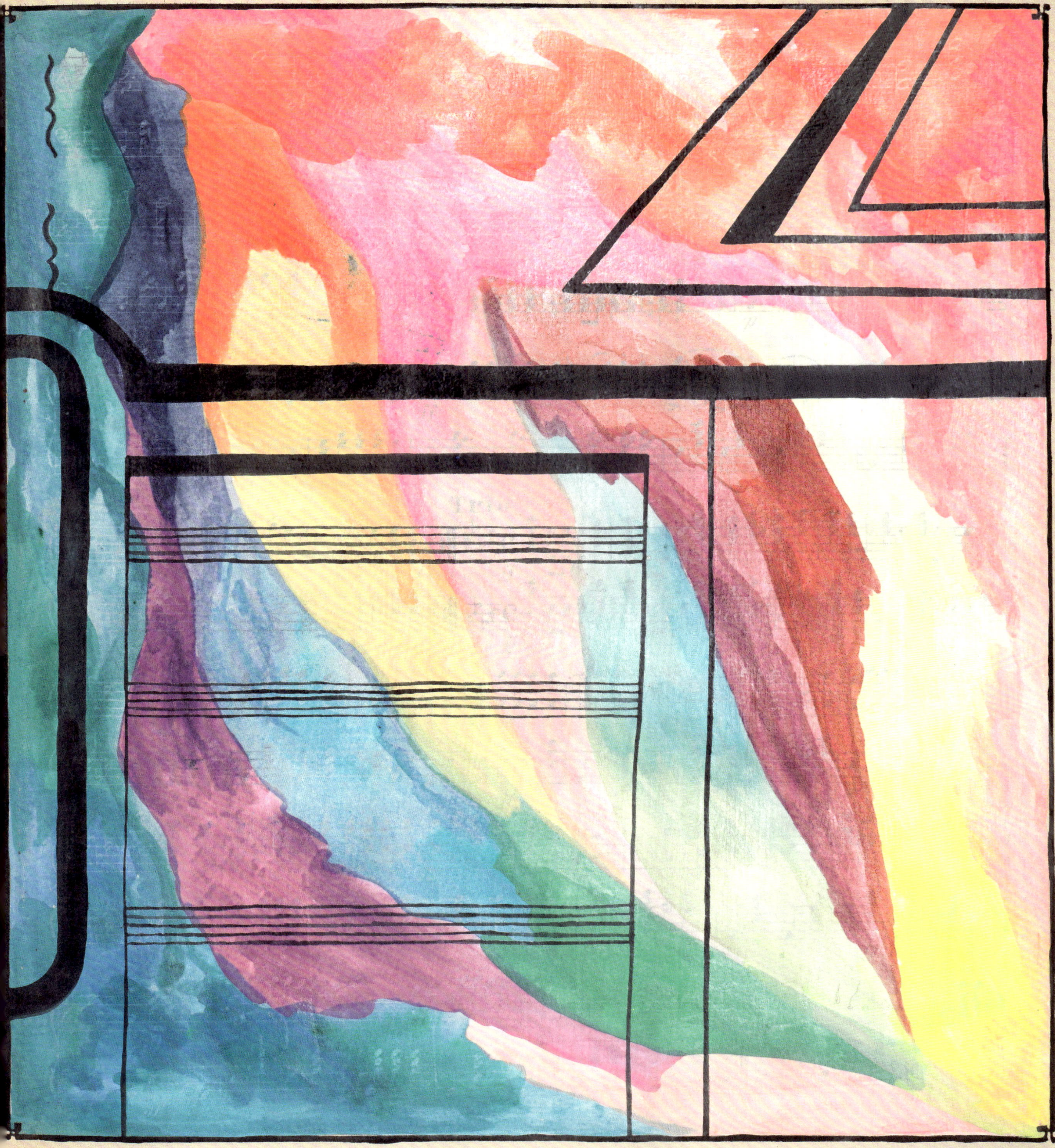

MARSCH ÜBER DAS BLÜCHER'SCHE SOLDATENLIED:

„Was blasen die Trompeten"

N° 2.

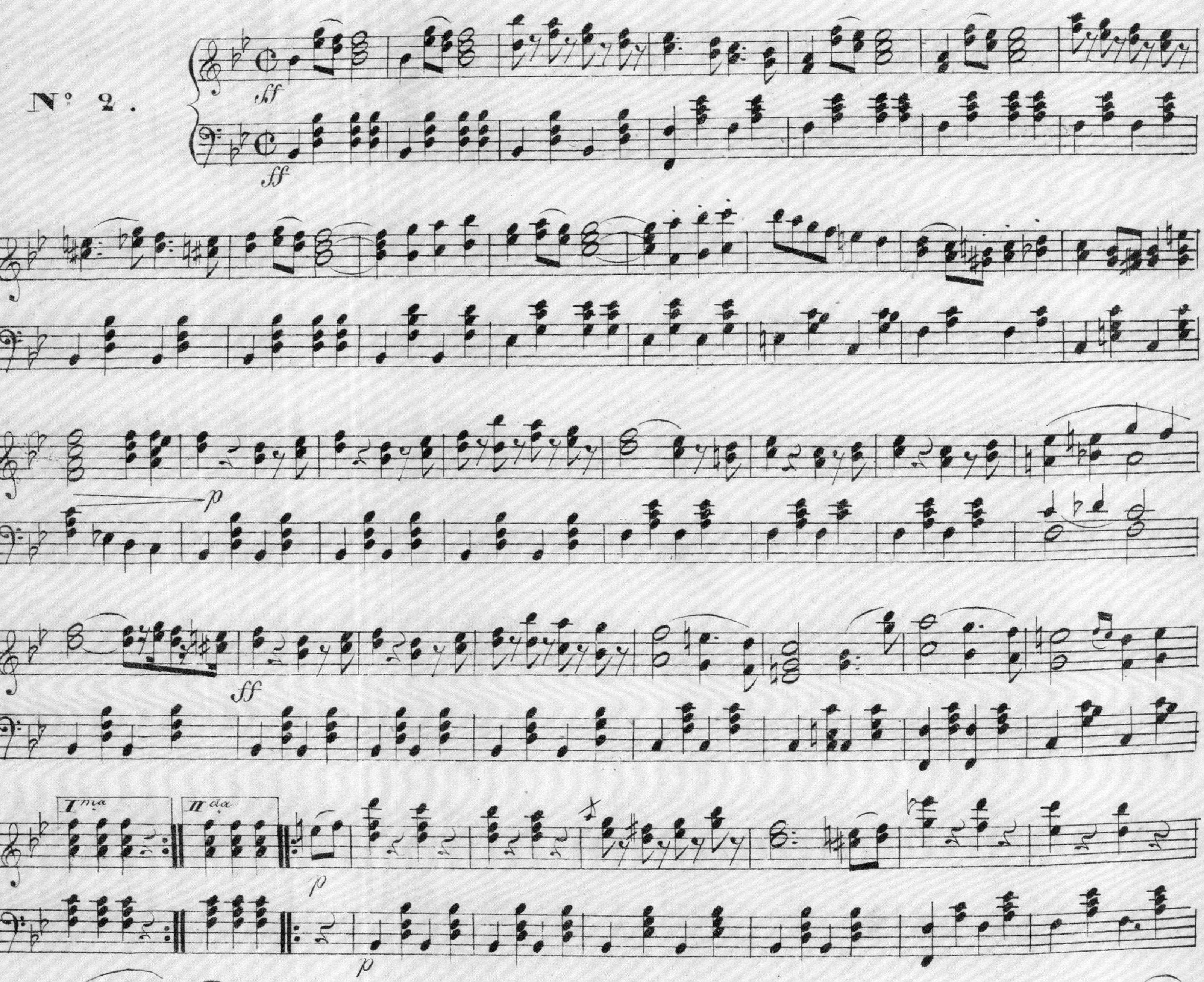

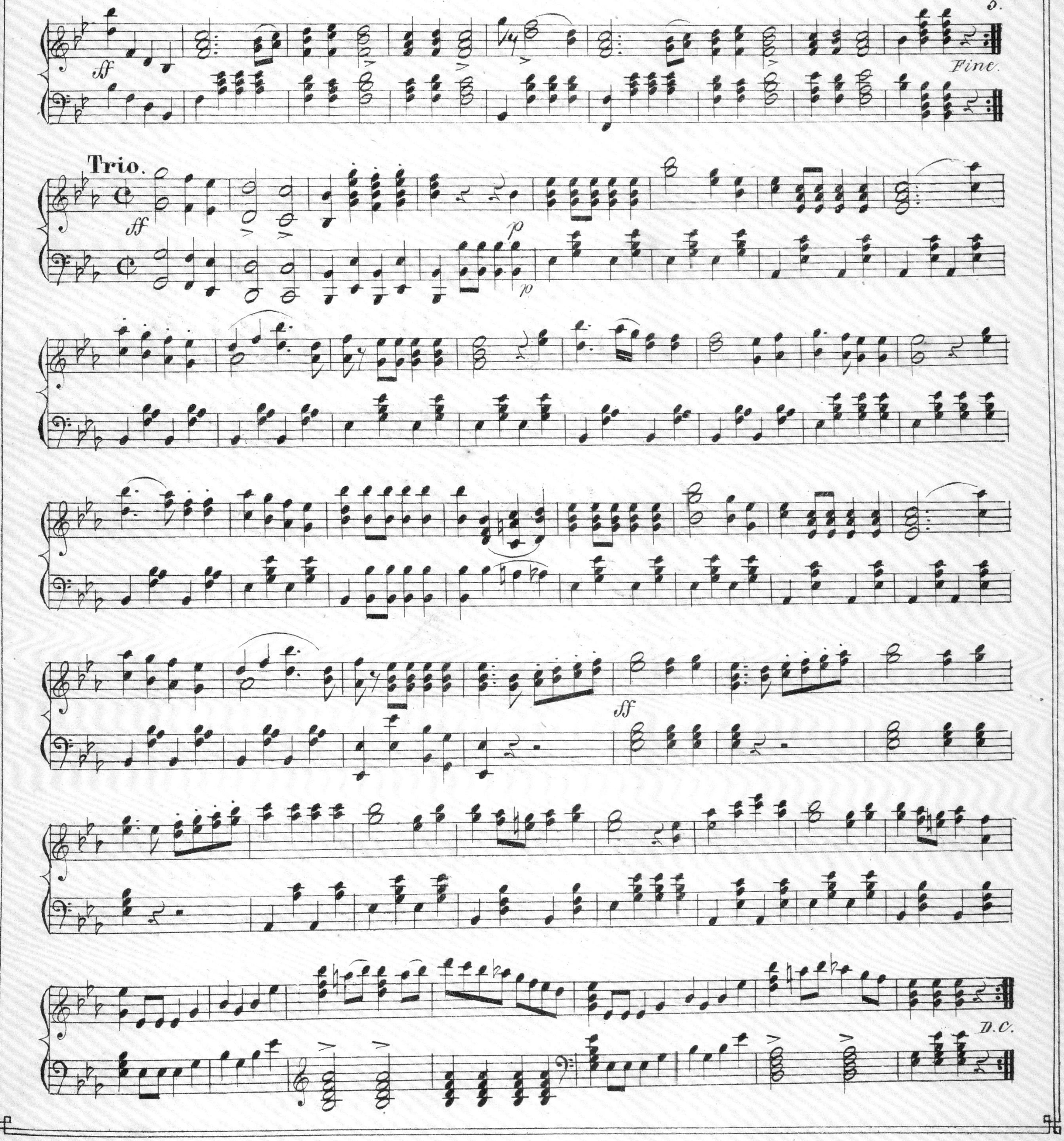
ff
Fine.
Trio.
ff
p
p
ff
D.C.

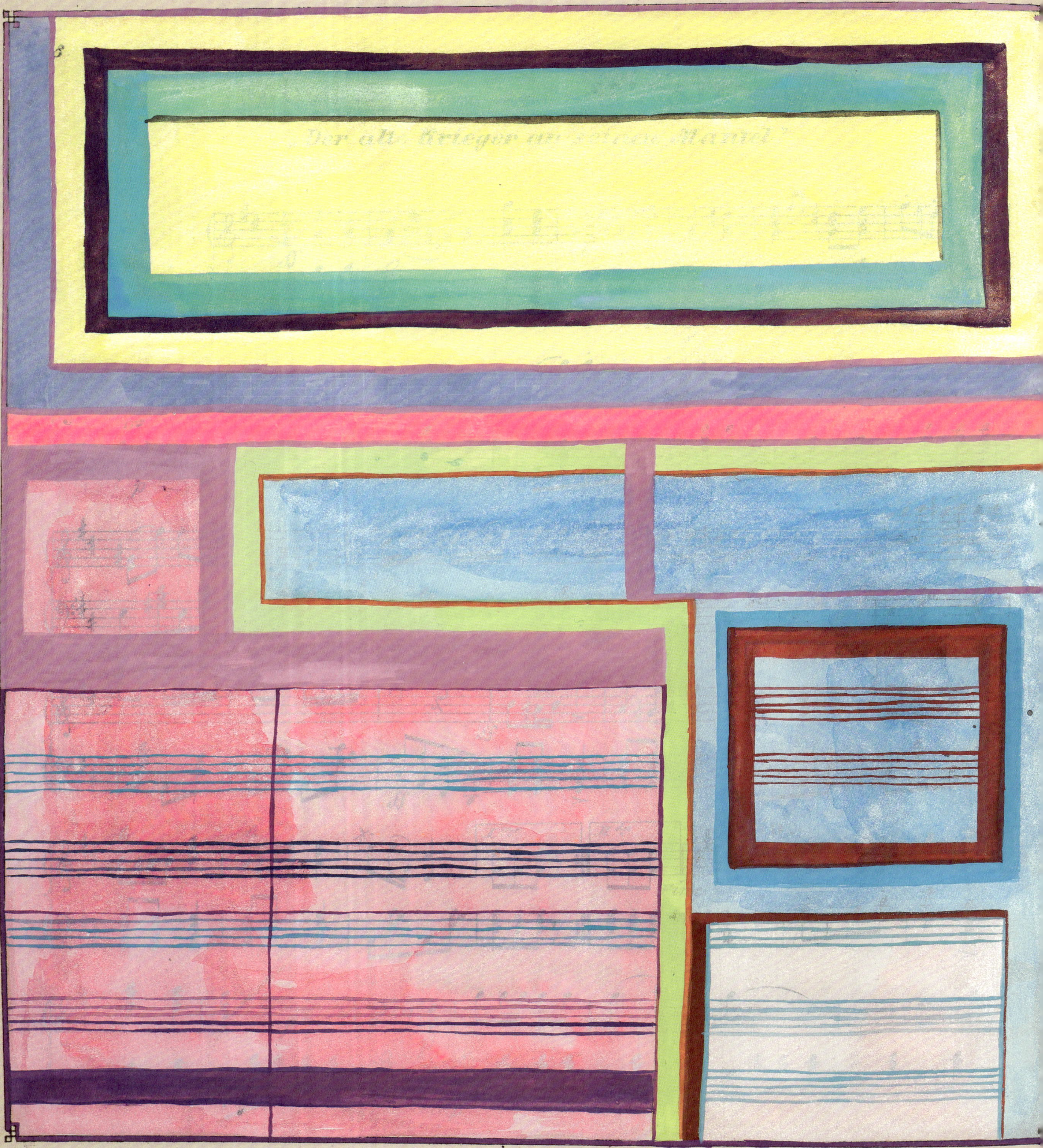

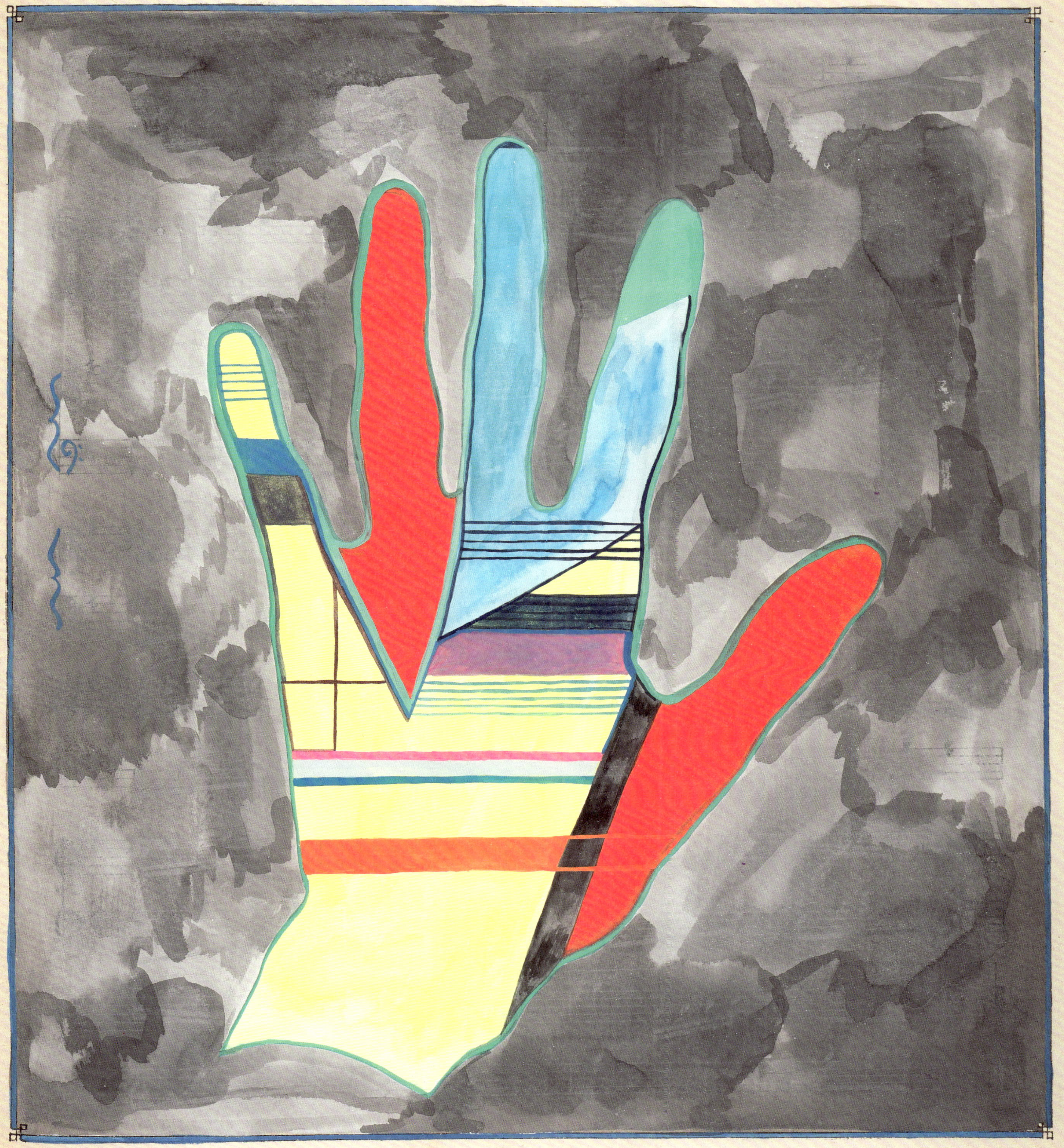

élégants

sur des motifs d'Opéras favoris

pour le

PIANO

par

Propriété de l'Editeur.

OFFENBACH s/M, chez JEAN ANDRÉ.

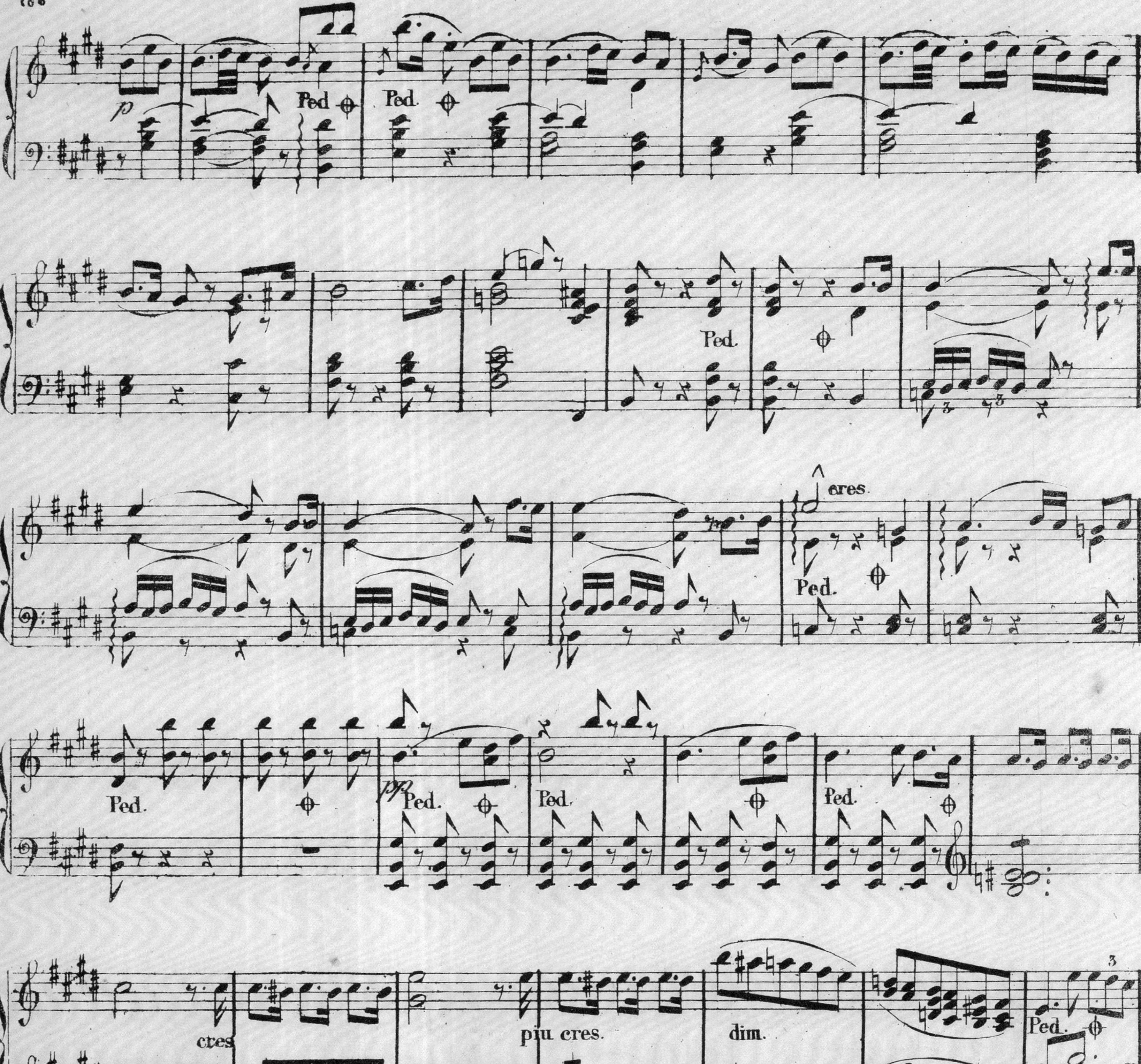
p
Ped
Ped.
cres.
pp
cres
piu cres.
dim.

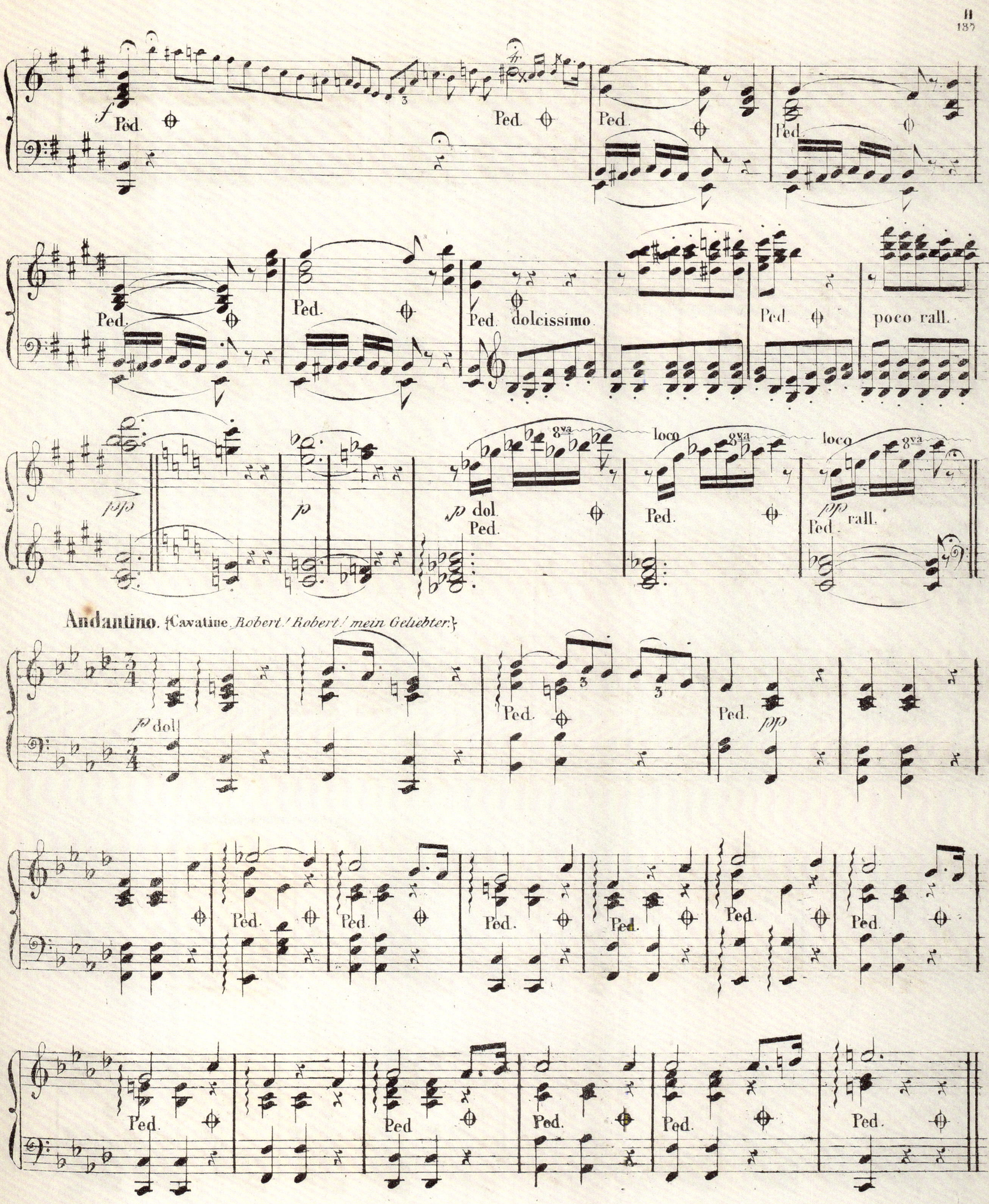
Ped.
dolcissimo
poco rall.
dol.
8va
loco
rall.
Andantino. (Cavatine Robert! Robert! mein Geliebter.)
dol.

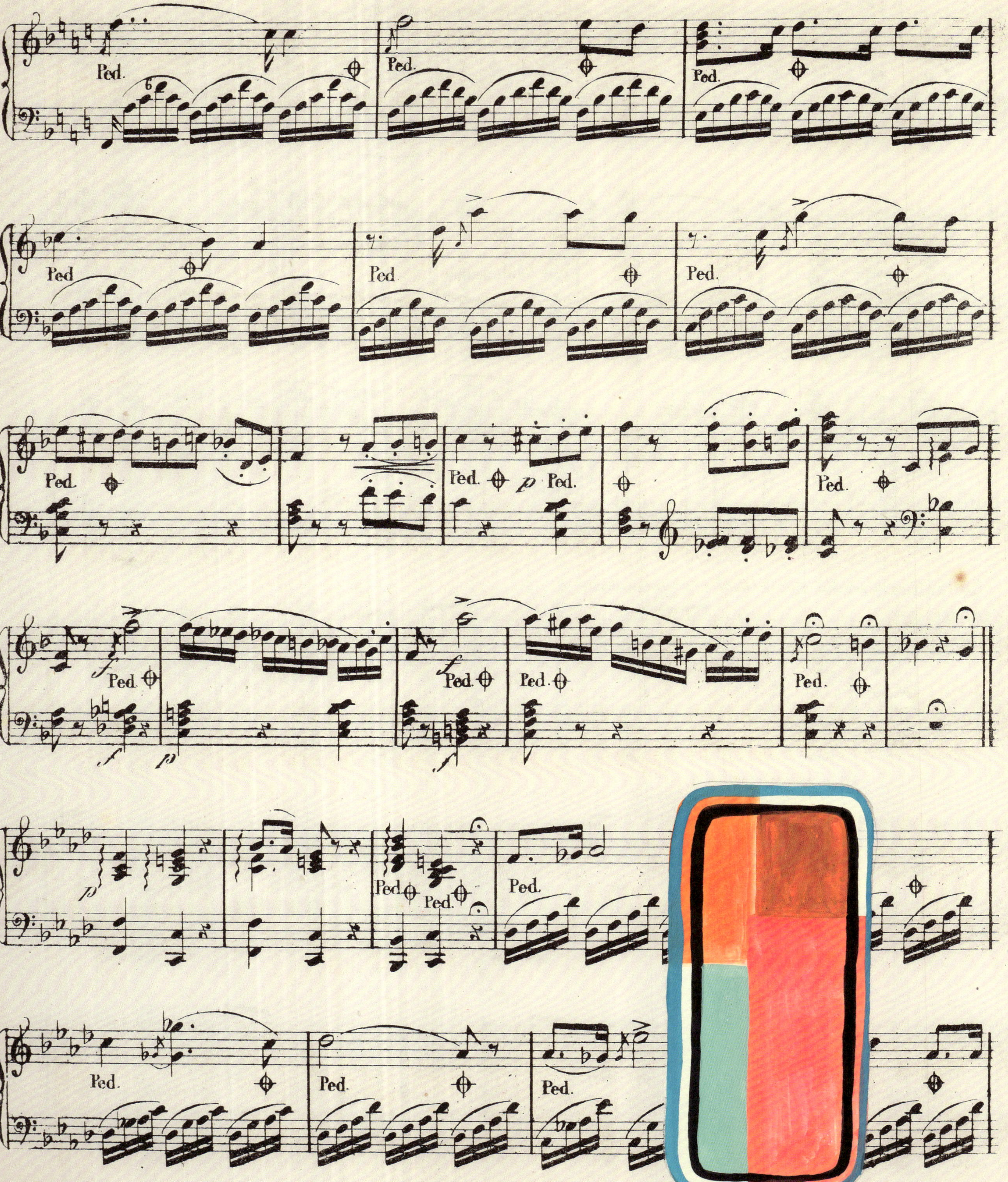
Ped.

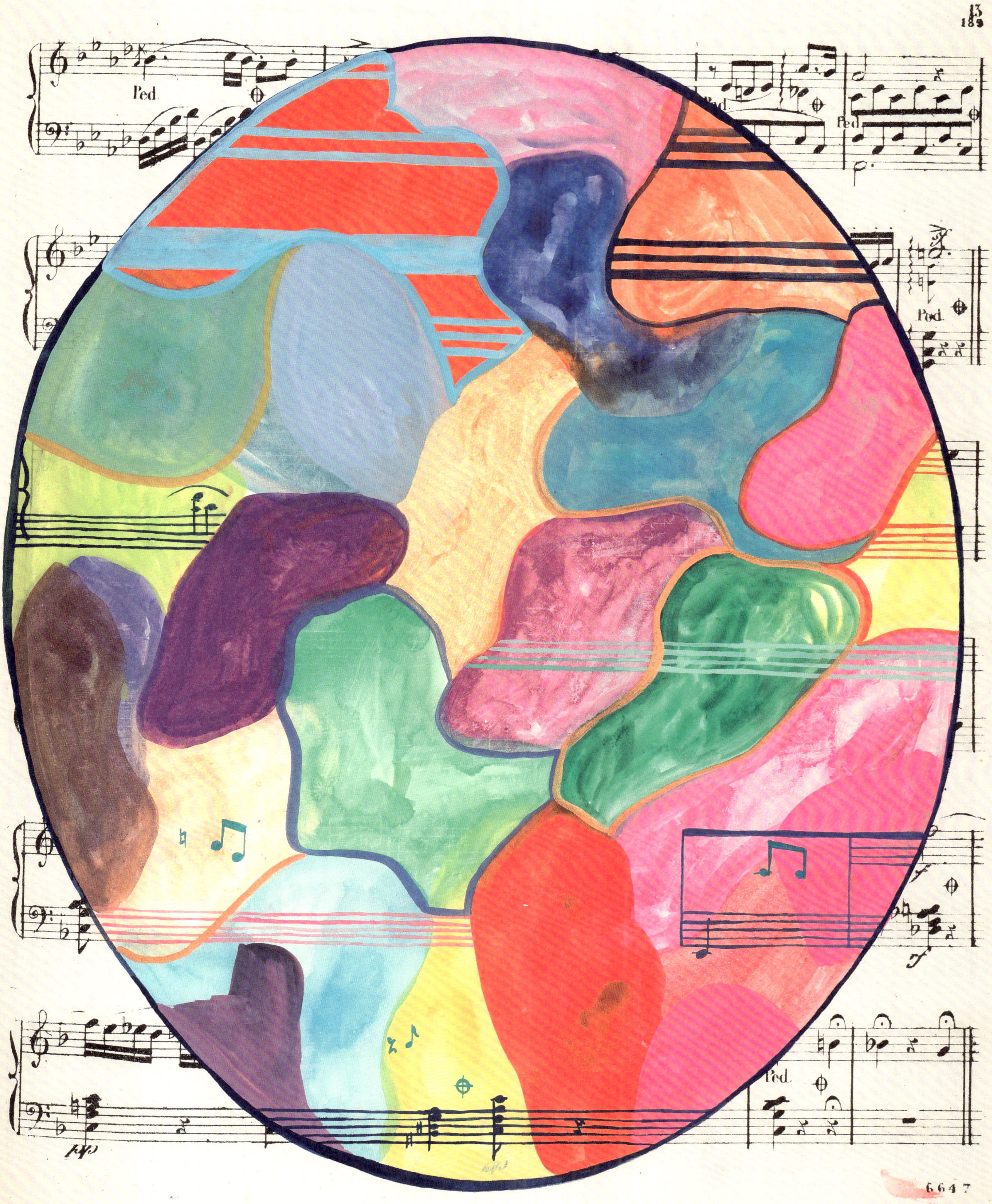
13
Ped.
Ped.
Ped.
Ped.
Ped.
pp
6647

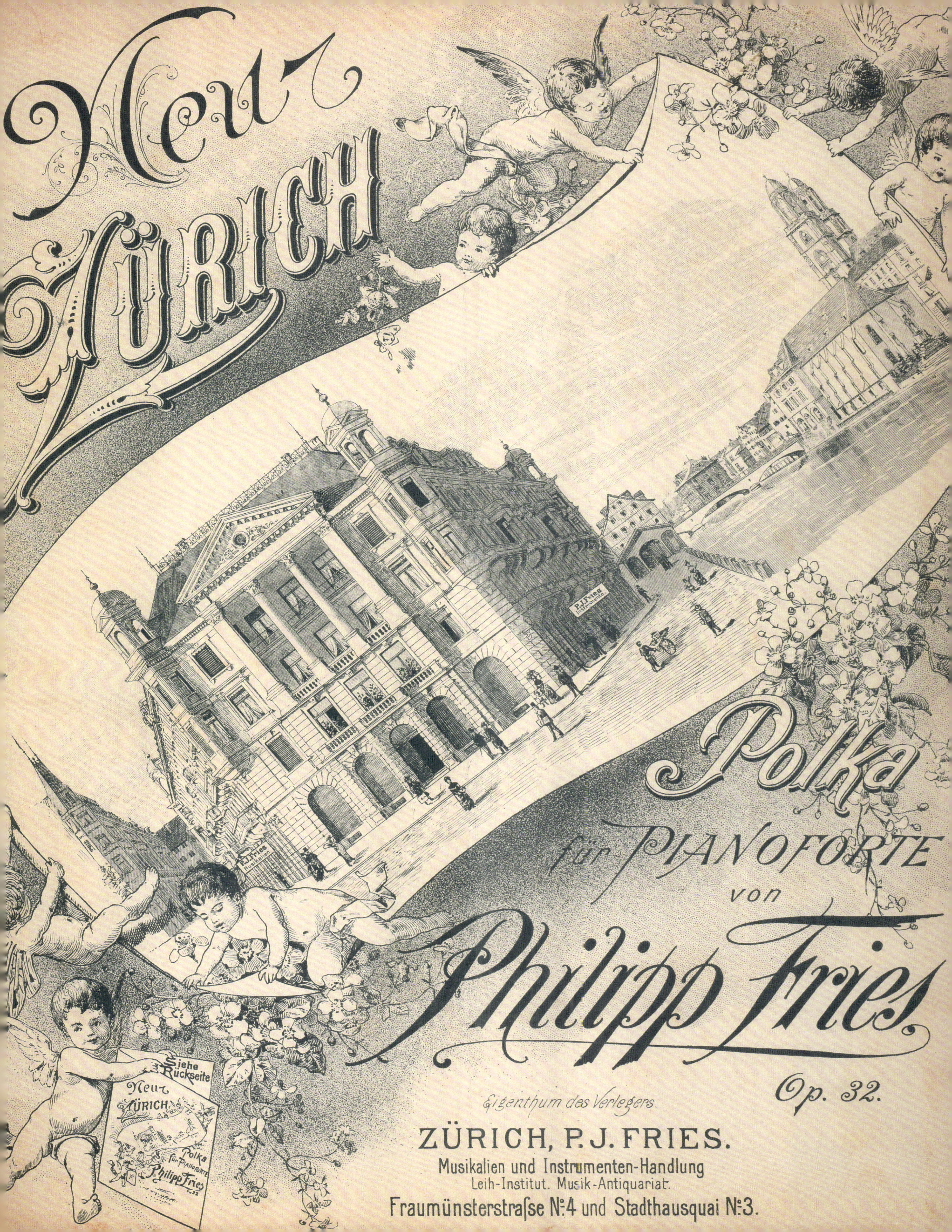
Neu Zürich
Polka
für PIANOFORTE
von
Philipp Fries
Op. 32.
Eigenthum des Verlegers.
ZÜRICH, P. J. FRIES.
Musikalien und Instrumenten-Handlung
Leih-Institut. Musik-Antiquariat.
Fraumünsterstrasse №4 und Stadthausquai №3.
Siehe Rückseite
Neu Zürich
Polka
für Pianoforte
Philipp Fries
P. J. Fries

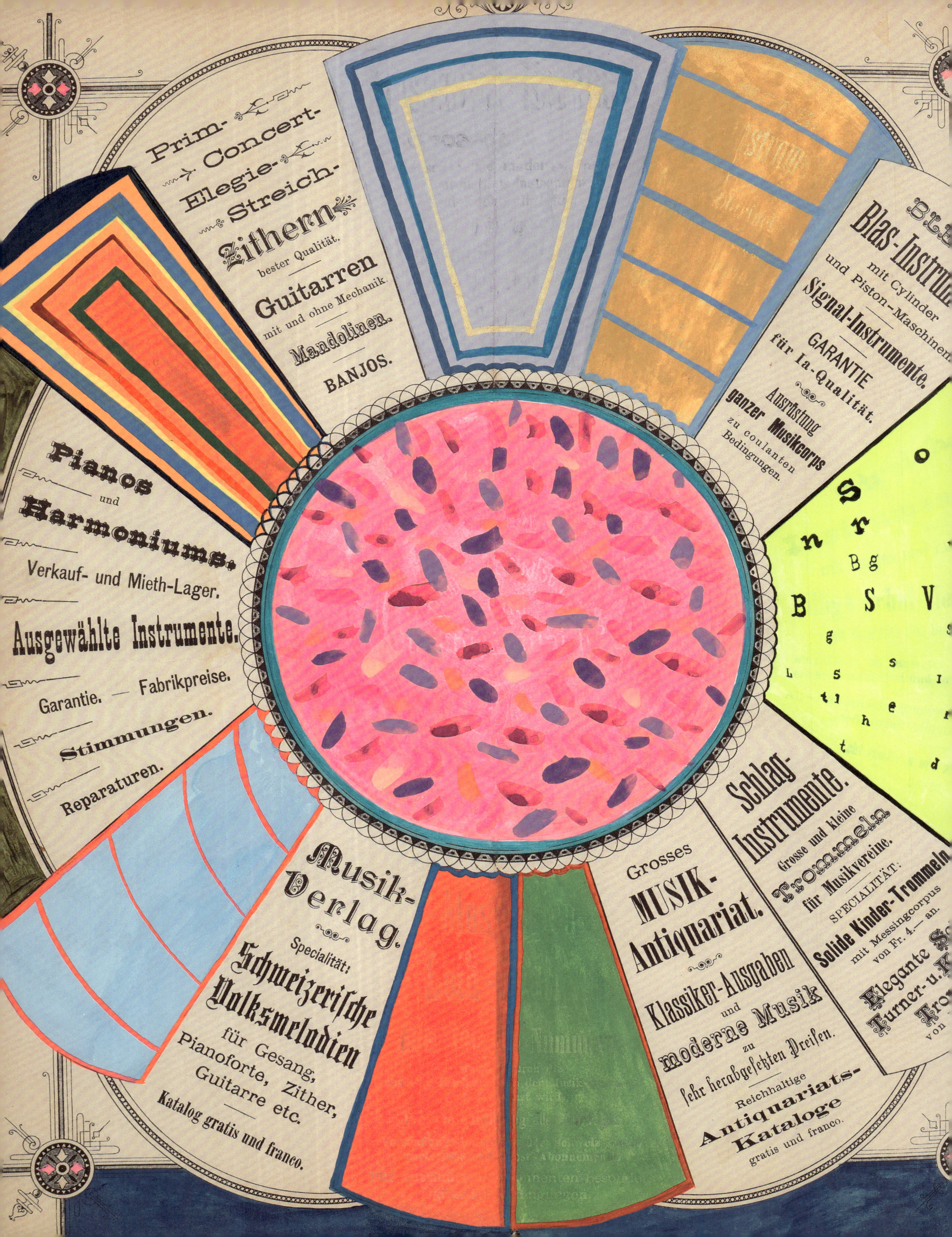
Prim- Concert- Elegie- Streich-
Zithern
bester Qualität.
Guitarren
mit und ohne Mechanik.
Mandolinen.
BANJOS.
Blas-Instrum
mit Cylinder und Piston-Maschinen
Signal-Instrumente.
GARANTIE
für Ia-Qualität.
Ausrüstung ganzer Musikcorps
zu coulanten Bedingungen.
Pianos
und
Harmoniums.
Verkauf- und Mieth-Lager.
Ausgewählte Instrumente.
Garantie. — Fabrikpreise.
Stimmungen.
Reparaturen.
Musik-Verlag.
Specialität:
Schweizerische Volksmelodien
für Gesang, Pianoforte, Zither, Guitarre etc.
Katalog gratis und franco.
Grosses
MUSIK-Antiquariat.
Klassiker-Ausgaben
und
moderne Musik
zu sehr herabgesetzten Preisen.
Reichhaltige
Antiquariats-Kataloge
gratis und franco.
Schlag-Instrumente.
Grosse und kleine
Trommeln
für Musikvereine.
SPECIALITÄT:
Solide Kinder-Trommeln
mit Messingcorpus
von Fr. 4.— an.

chorale grec.

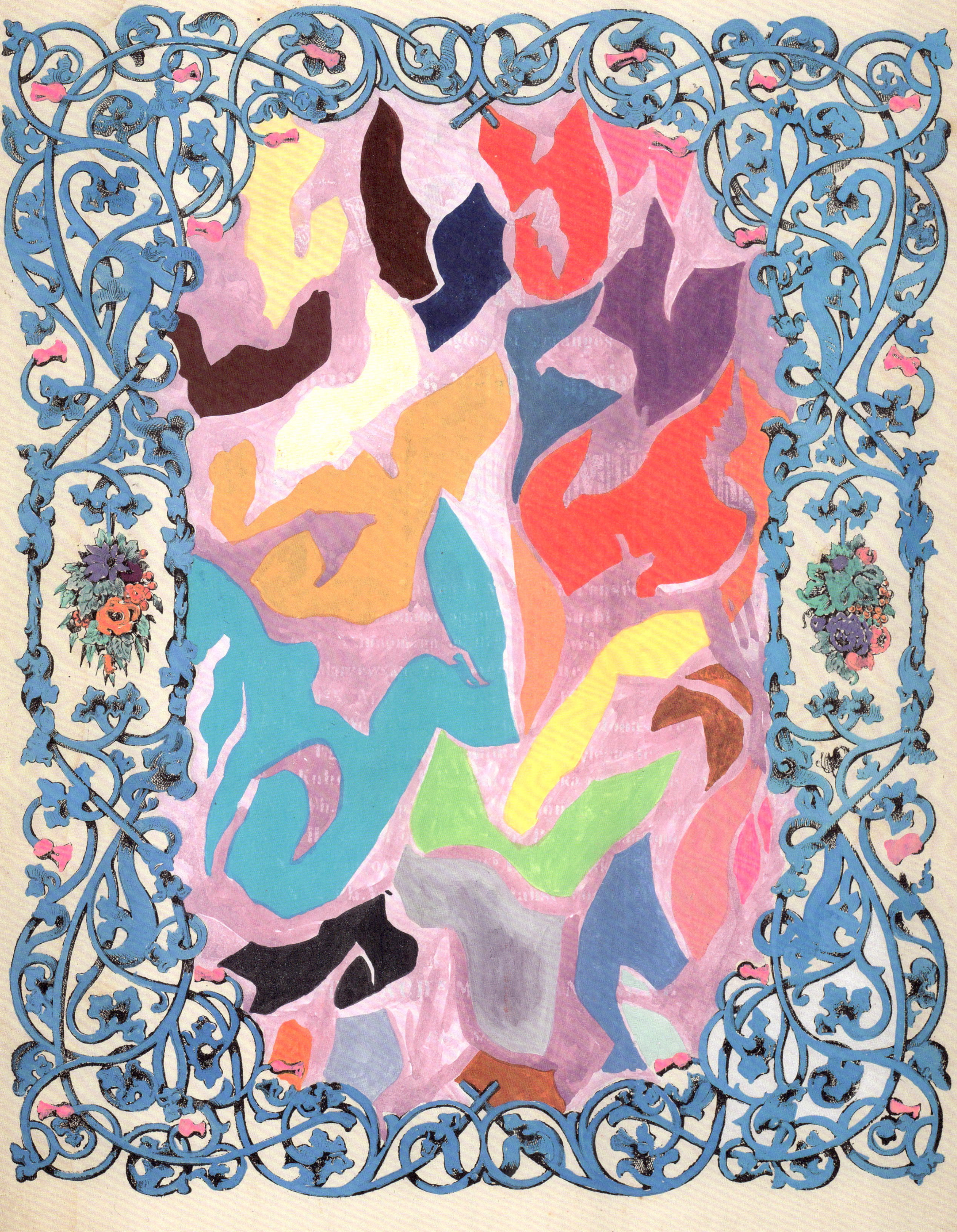

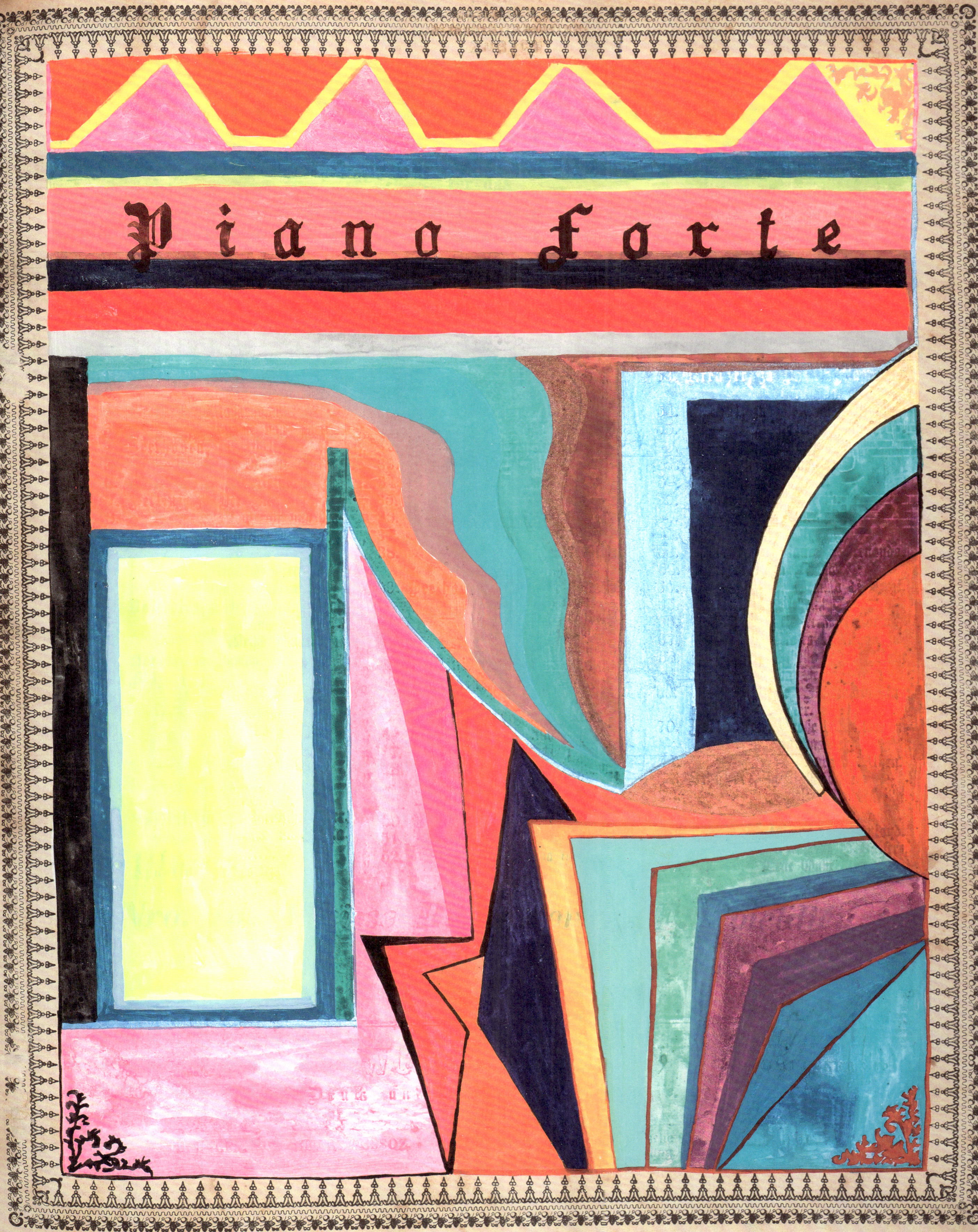
Piano Forte

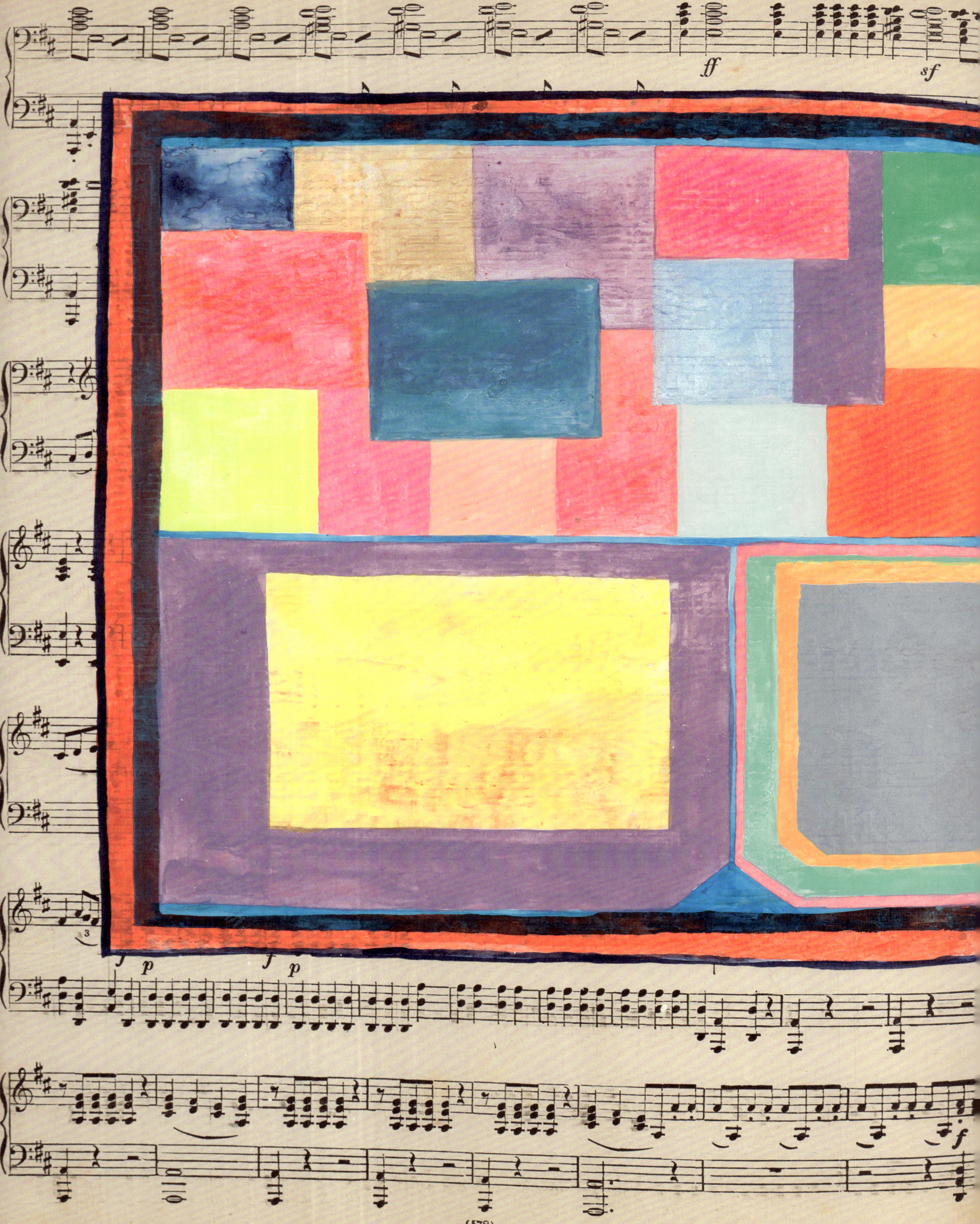
ff
sf
f p
f p
f

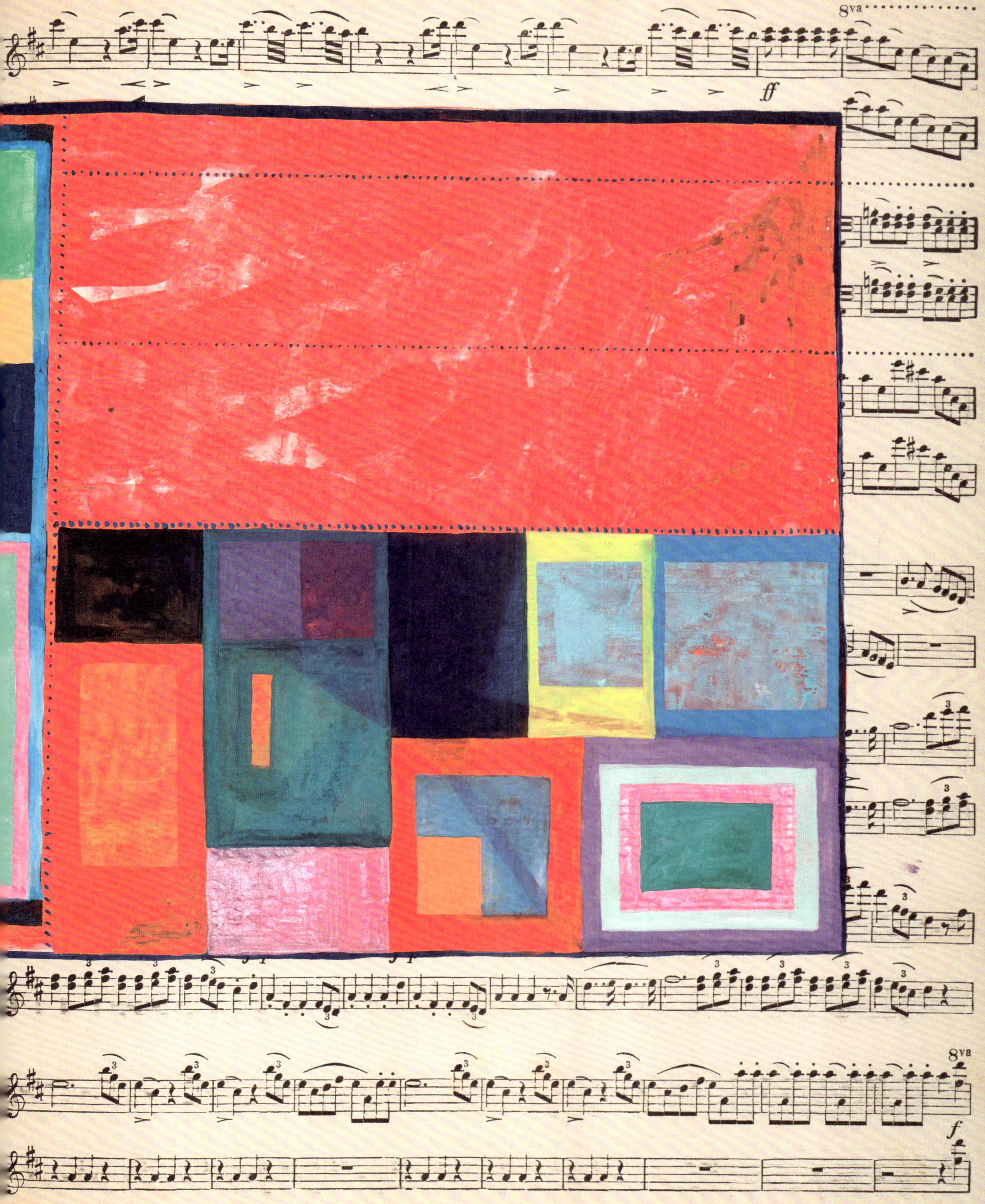
8va
ff
8va
f

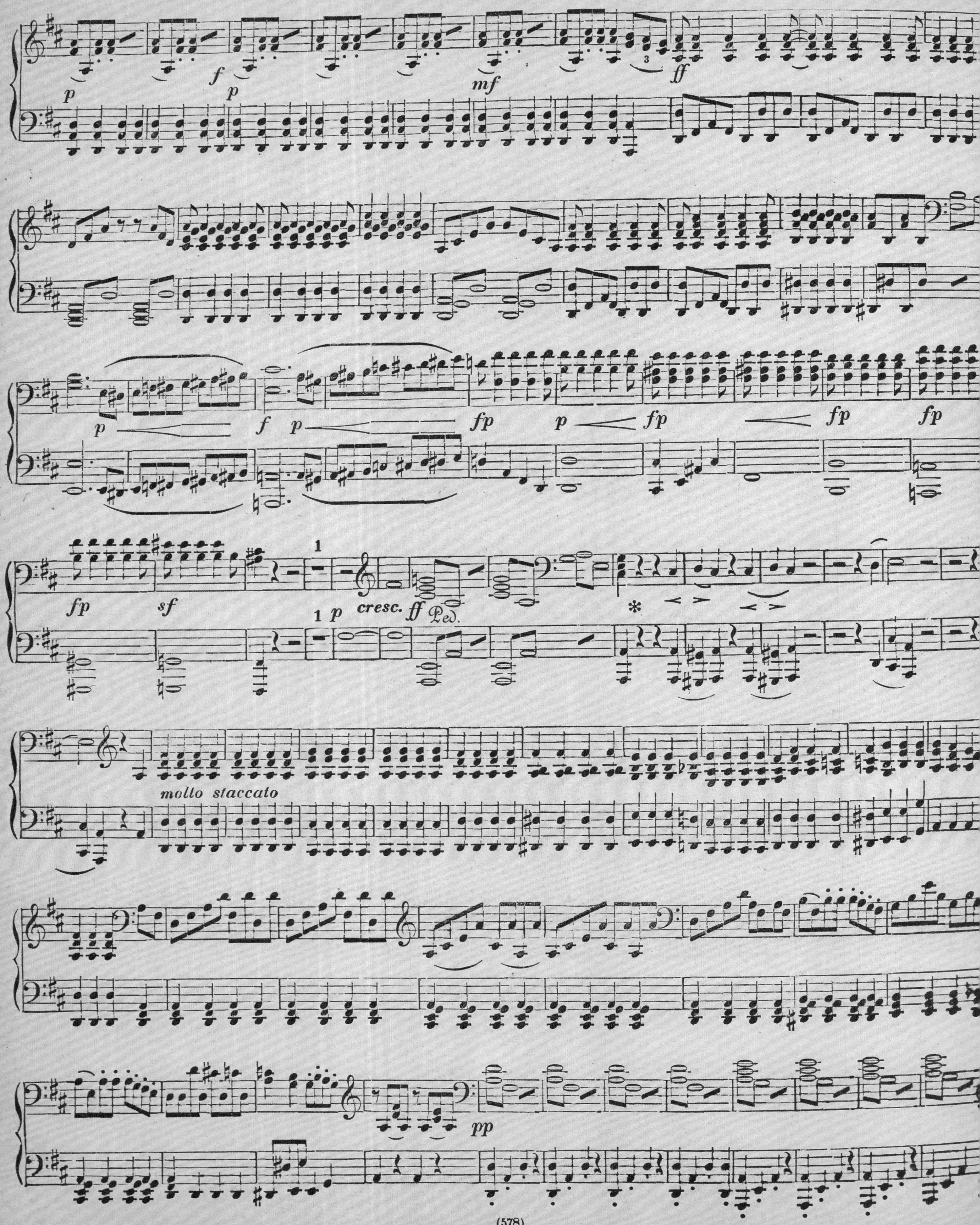
p
f
p
mf
ff
p
f
p
fp
p
fp
fp
fp
fp
sf
1
1 p
cresc.
ff
Ped.
molto staccato
pp

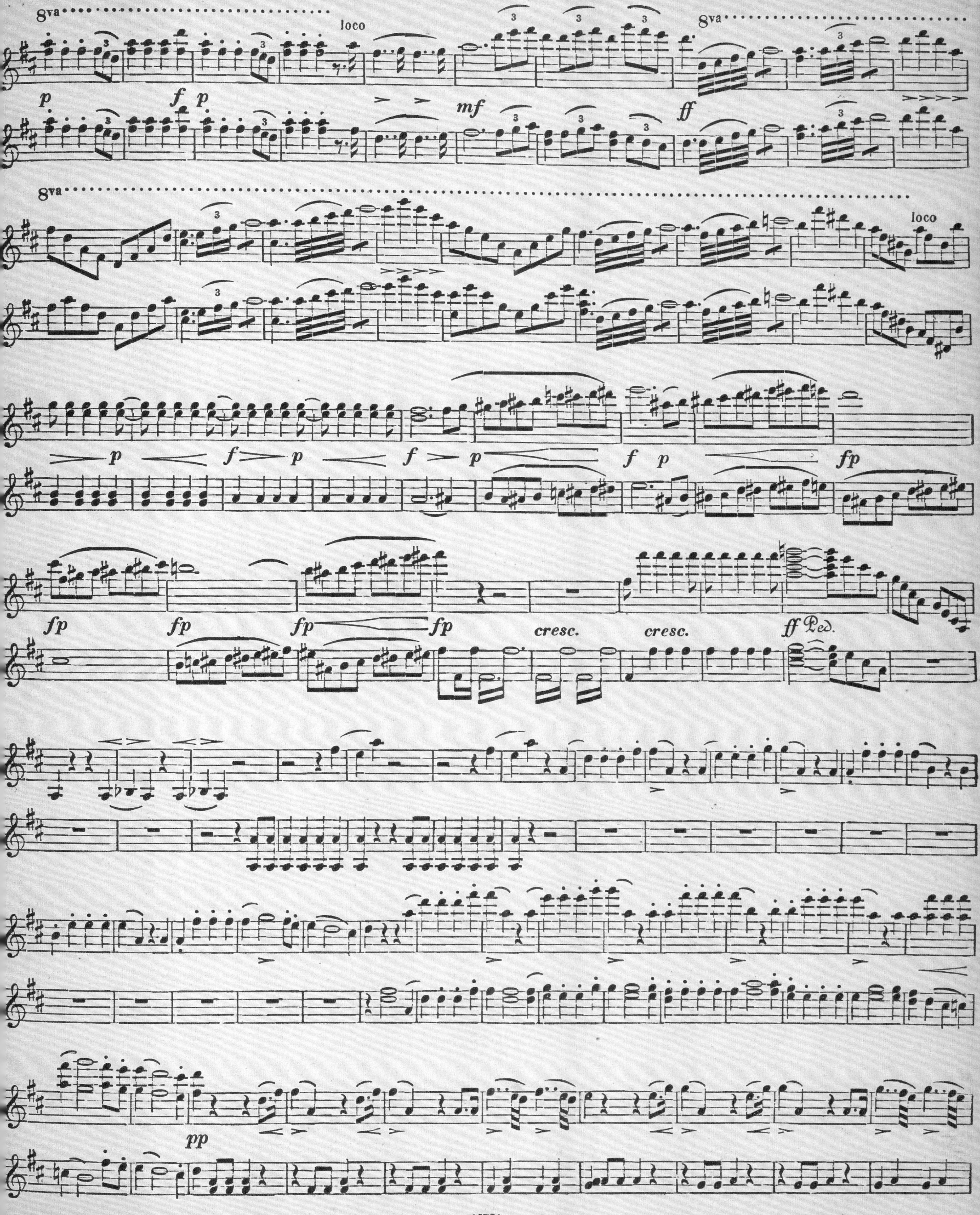
8va
loco
p
f
mf
ff
cresc.
fp
pp
Ped.

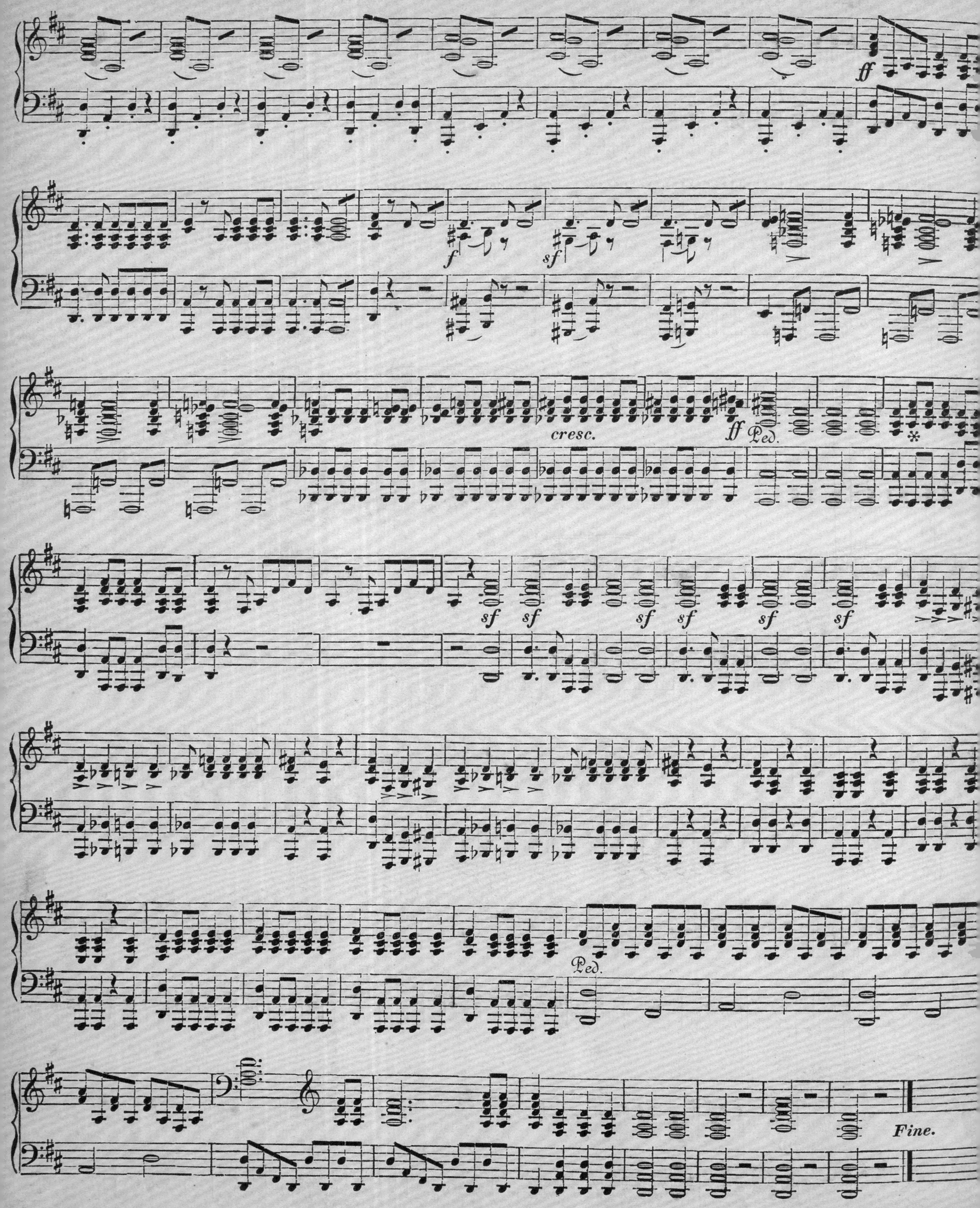
ff
f
sf
cresc.
ff
Ped.
sf
Ped.
Fine.

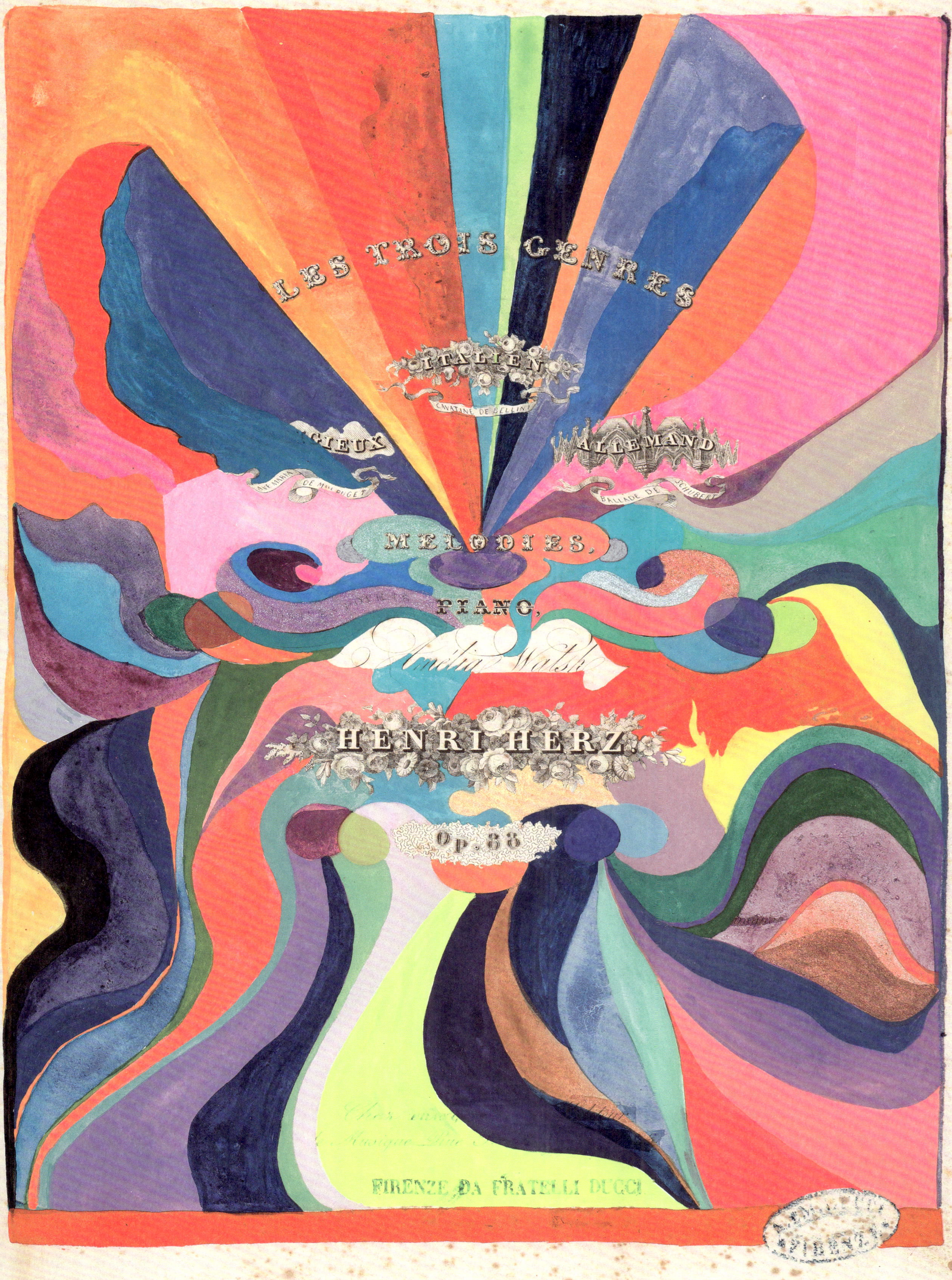
LES TROIS GENRES
ITALIEN
CAVATINE DE BELLINI
GIEUX
AVE MARIA DE Mlle PUGET
ALLEMAND
BALLADE DE SCHUBERT
MELODIES,
PIANO,
Amelia Walsh
HENRI HERZ.
Op. 88
FIRENZE DA FRATELLI DUCCI

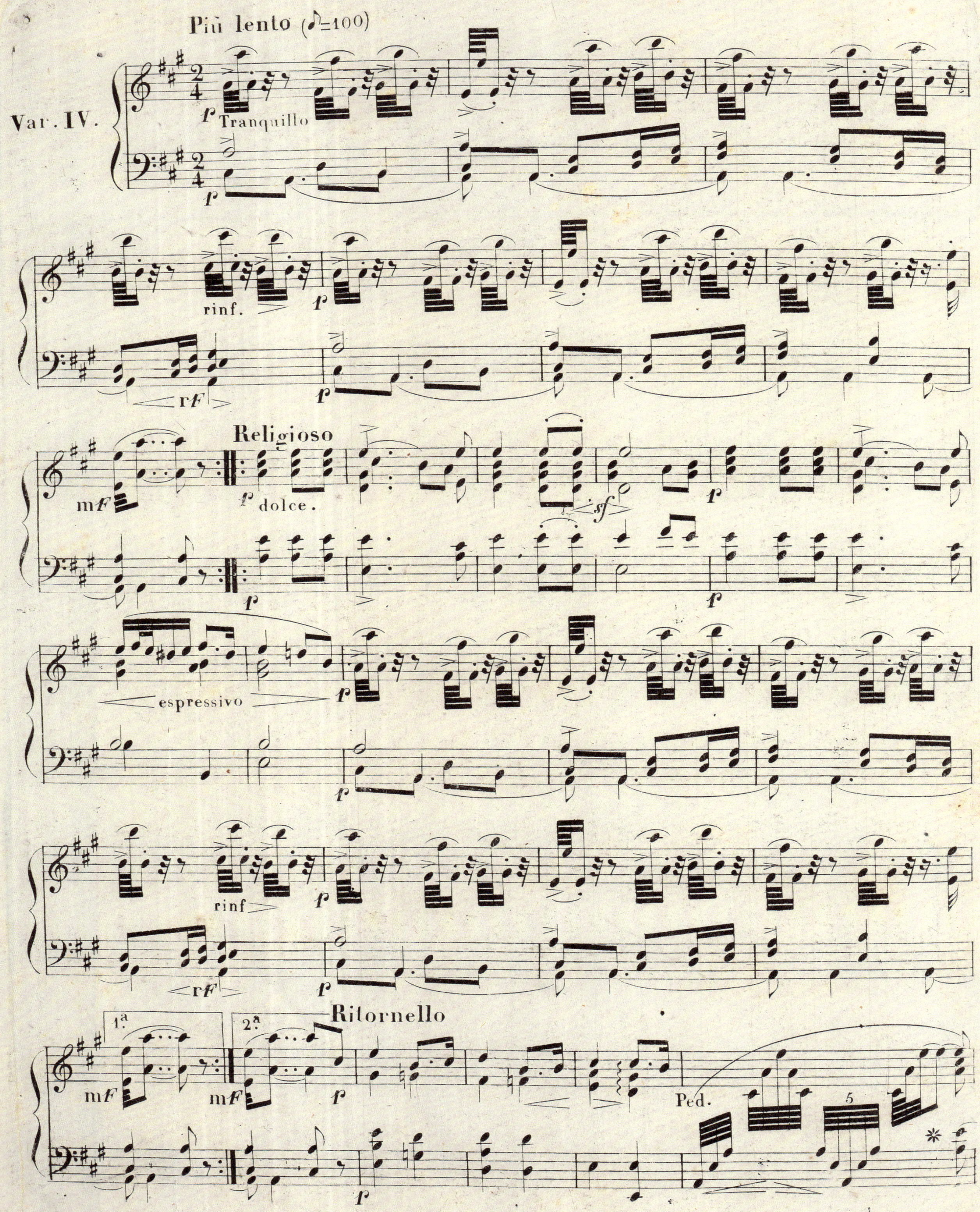
Più lento (♪=100)
Var. IV.
Tranquillo
rinf.
rf
Religioso
dolce.
sf
espressivo
1a
2a
Ritornello
Ped.

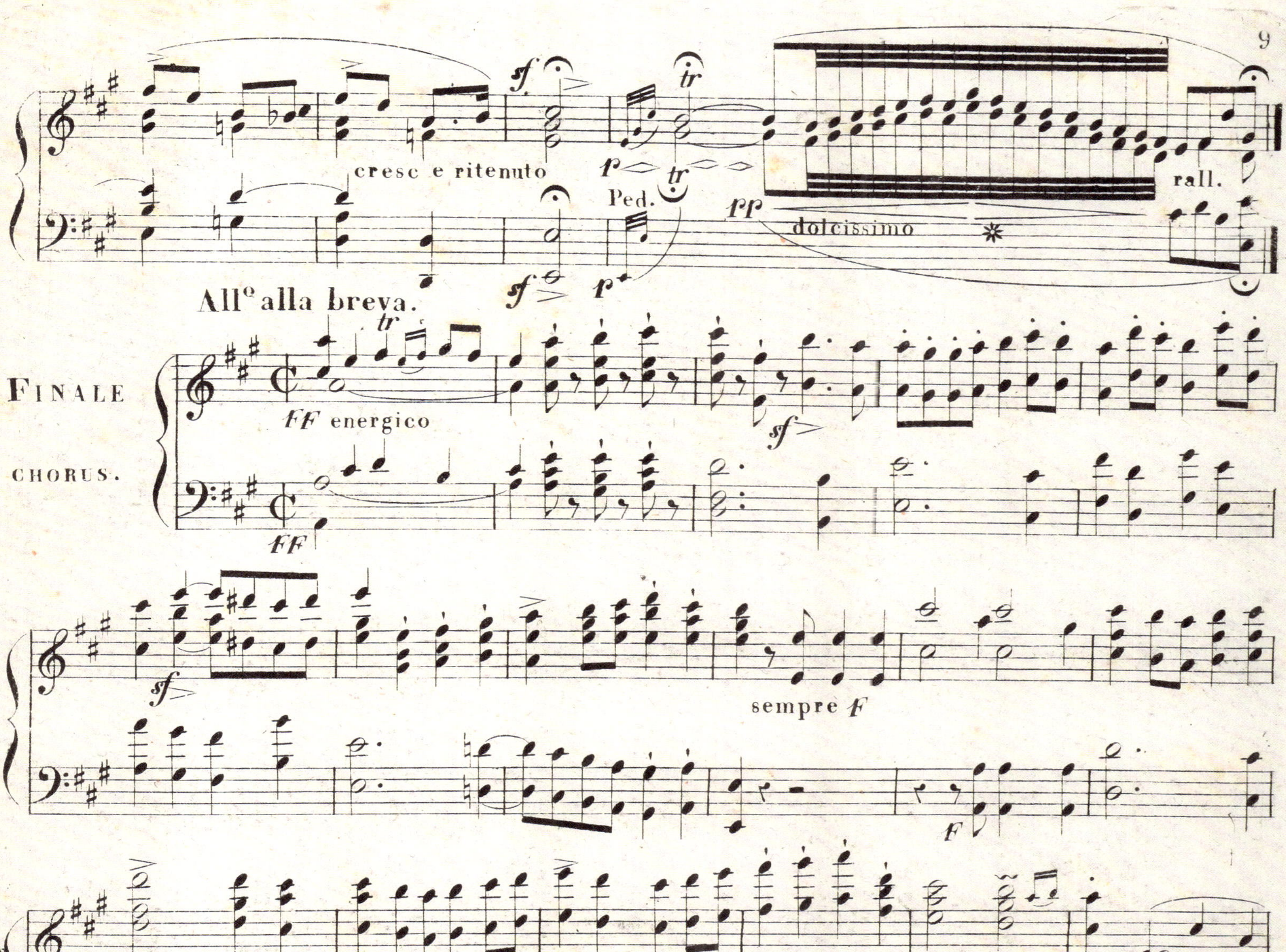
cresc e ritenuto
Ped.
dolcissimo
rall.
Allº alla breva.
FINALE
CHORUS.
energico
sempre F
dol.

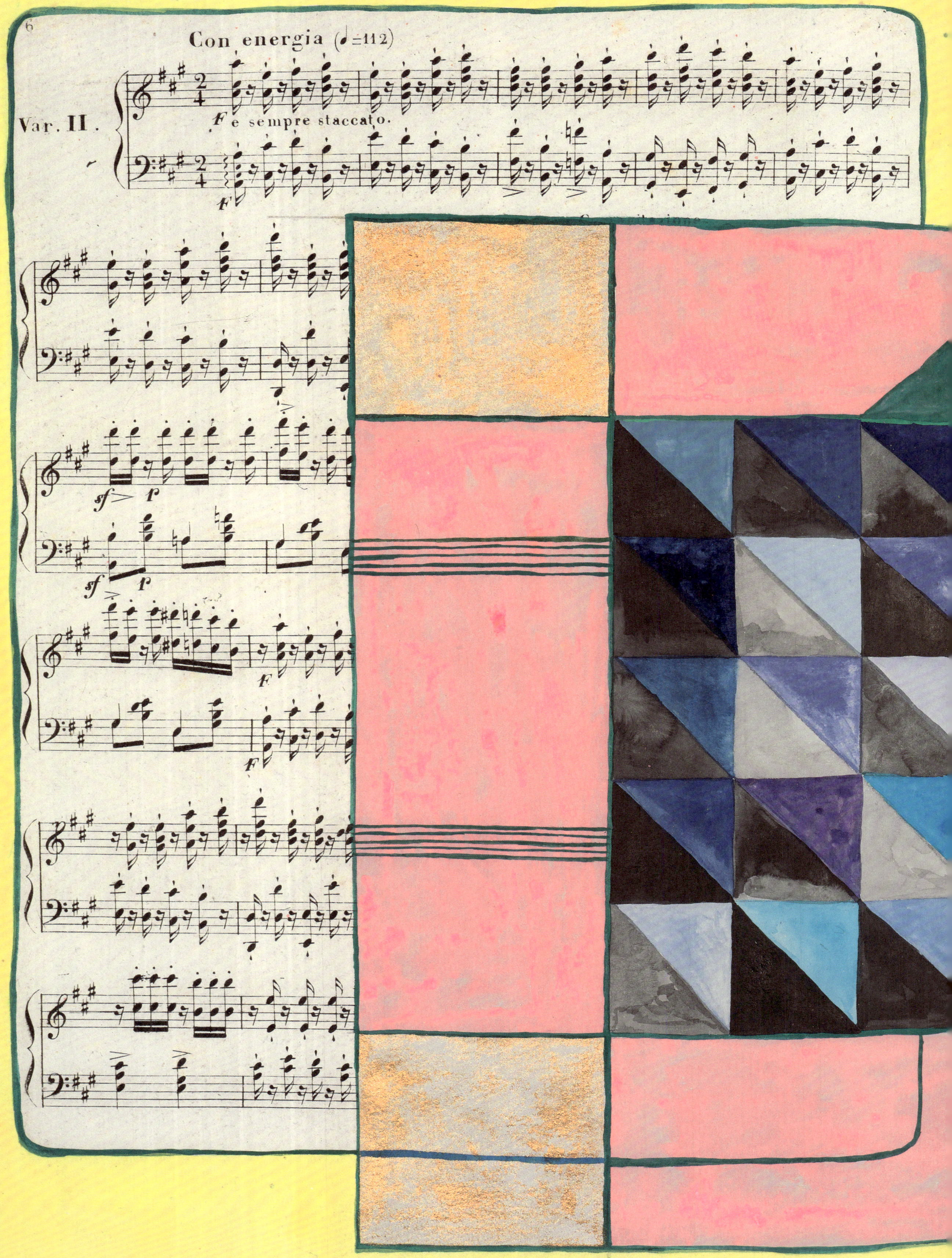
Con energia (♩=112)
Var. II.
F e sempre staccato.

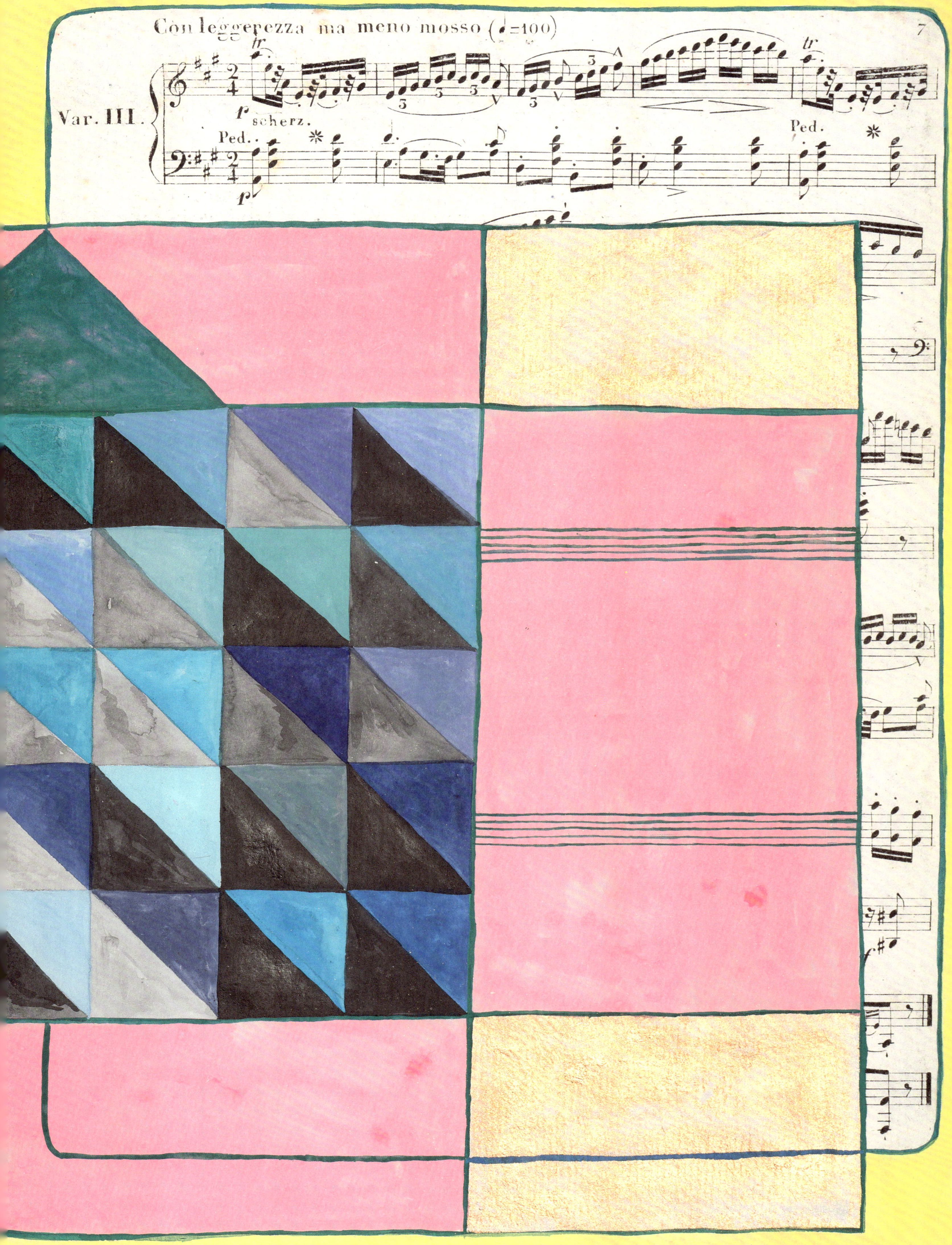
Con leggerezza ma meno mosso (♩=100)
7
Var. III.
scherz.
Ped.

I started this book in 2008. I had recently moved to Los Angeles.

I've carried this book through three studios. It is a record of time that I open, start, close, and put away, like a diary.

It is an object meant for the hand.

Works on paper are meditative for me. When I travel to make a work on-site, the first thing I do when I get back to the studio is return to one of these pages. This book grounds me. Painting on the scores reminds me of the freedom of being in a country where you don't speak the language, when language opens up to many possible translations.

I like to find things that are already there and react to them. This book was found in a thrift store in Zurich. Everything is a response to something else. Sometimes I think every minute in life is a collage — how you get dressed in the morning, who you sit next to at a dinner party — it all dictates the next part.

Sarah Cain

Sarah Cain
Music Book

Editors: Ian Berry and Sarah Cain
Design: Purtill Family Business
Photography: Jeff McLane
Color separations: Echelon, Los Angeles
Printing and binding: Conti Tipocolor

First edition of 1,000 copies published in June 2021 by The Frances Young Tang Teaching Museum and Art Gallery, Skidmore College, Saratoga Springs, NY, and X Artists' Books, Los Angeles, CA.

Typeset in Akkurat and printed on Munken Pure.

Library of Congress Cataloging-in-Publication Data is available on request.

ISBN 978-0-9988616-9-2

All images in this book are by Sarah Cain, gouache and acrylic on found paper, 2008–2021

Special thanks to Maddie Klett for her interview with Sarah Cain, originally published in *BOMB* magazine, from which the artist's statement is drawn.

This publication accompanies the exhibition

Sarah Cain
Enter the Center

The Frances Young Tang Teaching Museum and Art Gallery
Skidmore College
July 10, 2021 – January 2, 2022

tang

The Frances Young Tang Teaching Museum and Art Gallery
Skidmore College
815 N. Broadway
Saratoga Springs, NY 12866
https://tang.skidmore.edu

X ARTISTS' BOOKS

X Artists' Books
PO Box 3424
South Pasadena, CA 91031
www.xartistsbooks.com